DR. GARY SMALLEY
TED CUNNINGHAM

The Language of Sex

*experiencing the beauty
of sexual intimacy*

Regal

**From Gospel Light
Ventura, California, U.S.A.**

Published by Regal
From Gospel Light
Ventura, California, U.S.A.
www.regalbooks.com
Printed in the U.S.A.

Charts on pages 54 and 55 and "The Brain Sex Test" on pages 57-59 are reprinted by arrangement with Citadel Press, an imprint of Kensington Publishing Corporation (www.kensingtonbooks.com). All rights reserved.

Library of Congress Cataloging-in-Publication Data
Smalley, Gary.
  The language of sex / Gary Smalley and Ted Cunningham.
    p. cm.
  ISBN 978-0-8307-4568-5 (hard cover) — ISBN 978-0-8307-4623-1 (international trade paper)
  1. Sex—Religious aspects—Christianity. I. Cunningham, Ted. II. Title.
  BT708.S625 2008
  241'.66—dc22

                                                                                    2007034014

1 2 3 4 5 6 7 8 9 10 / 10 09 08

Rights for publishing this book outside the U.S.A. or in non-English languages are administered by Gospel Light Worldwide, an international not-for-profit ministry. For additional information, please visit www.glww.org, email info@glww.org, or write to Gospel Light Worldwide, 1957 Eastman Avenue, Ventura, CA 93003, U.S.A.

Gary's Dedication:

*I dedicate this book to my daughter Kari and her husband,
Roger Thomas Gibson. Roger is not only my literary agent
but also a very close friend and an outstanding husband and father.
I'm sorry, dads across the world, but no father could possibly have a
better son-in-law. And I can't imagine any father having a more
loving, caring daughter, who not only is a wonderful mother but who
will also soon adopt a precious little girl, Zoie, from Ethiopia.*

Ted's Dedication:

*I dedicate this book to my lover, bride and best friend, Amy.
My love for her increases each day. We have big dreams for life together.
She is a great mom and a gifted children's director at our church.
I not only get to spend time at home with her, but I get to work with
her as well. She is my biggest fan, and I am hers!
I love you, Amy!*

Contents

Acknowledgments

We would like to thank Roger Gibson for dreaming with us and making *The Language of Sex* a reality. He serves as more than our literary agent; he is also a great friend.

Margaret Feinberg is much more than just a writer. She is a great collaborator with a journalistic style that draws the best out of us. Margaret is a servant and an incredible wordsmith.

A big thank-you to Alex Field for leading this book from start to finish at Regal. He has been so encouraging and is a pure delight to work with.

Thank you, Regal and Gospel Light! Bill Greig III, you lead your team with excellence. Also, a big thanks goes to the team, including Bill Denzel, Bruce Barbour, Mark Weising, Aly Hawkins and the marketing and sales teams at Regal Books!

We also want to say thank you to all of the staff at the Smalley Relationship Center. Day in and day out, you serve marriages around the world. Your hard work does not go unnoticed. Thank you.

Thank you, Norma Smalley, Terry Brown, Ron Cunningham, Bonnie Cunningham, Scott Weatherford, Austin Deloach, Kim Fertig, Sue Parks and Roger Gibson for reading the manuscript and offering great insight.

The staff at Woodland Hills Community Church played a big part in this book. Ted Burden and Bernard Bourque offered many valuable teaching insights. Pam Strayer transcribed, and Denise Bevins handled so many details of my life during the process. Richard Williams and Jim Brawner helped with creative process. Thank you! Thank you! Thank you!

To all of our family and friends, many of whom have stories that fill these pages, we love you and owe you a debt of gratitude for the patience in this process.

Preface

This is my (Gary's) first book with Ted Cunningham. I have known Ted and his wife, Amy, for six years. He's a great husband and a father of two wonderful kids, Corynn and Carson. Not only is Ted my dear friend and a great writer and communicator, but he is also my pastor. Ted and I have served as elders together at Woodland Hills Church in Branson, Missouri, for over six years now. Each week, my wife, Norma, and I are thrilled to see how God uses Ted to reach thousands in our community. His messages are so practical and vulnerable. I have learned much from Ted and have thoroughly enjoyed writing this book with him. I know you will learn much from him, too.

(Just so you know: The names of those mentioned throughout this book as well as the details of the stories have been changed in order to protect the identities as well as the relationships of those involved.)

The Language of Sex

CHAPTER 1

The Foundation for the Best Sex

As a recent bride, Ellen was more than a little nervous walking into church. Raised in a healthy, faith-based home, her parents had recently celebrated their thirty-fifth wedding anniversary. Ellen had never expected to find herself in need of counseling for herself—let alone for her marriage.

As she sat in the office waiting area, she caught herself twirling her medium-length blonde hair around her index finger, a habit she had developed as a child that unconsciously returned whenever she felt uneasy or upset. Suddenly aware of her behavior, she clasped her hands together firmly on her lap. She knew she had to talk to someone about what was really going on in her marriage. The pastor who married them seemed like the best choice.

The next few minutes felt like a bit of a blur. The secretary called Ellen's name. She stood up and walked down a long hallway where she was greeted by the pastor's firm handshake. She took a seat in a slightly oversized, well-worn leather chair.

"Where would you like to begin?" the pastor asked.

Ellen took a short quick breath. "We've been married for five years and we have sex two to three times a week," she said with a calmness that surprised her.

"That seems healthy and good," the pastor responded.

"But . . ." she looked down at the floor, struggling to find the right words or at least the courage to say them, "I have yet to experience an orgasm."

Tears welled up in her eyes. Like a bursting floodgate, she could no longer hold them back. "What am I doing wrong? What is he doing wrong? What are we doing wrong?" Ellen said, wiping warm droplets from her cheeks with the back of her hand.

The pastor looked at Ellen. He saw her pain. He could even feel a hint of the ache inside himself. But he had no response. Seminary had taught him a lot of great theology, but this question never came up in class. A string of thoughts bombarded his mind at once: *How could this young woman's husband have sex some 300 to 400 times and not get a response from his wife? How confused and even guilty must she feel after sex? What did their parents forget to tell them? Should I pull the young man aside and draw him some pictures? Is this an appropriate question to be asking a pastor? Is this an appropriate question for a pastor to be answering? Should I refer them to someone else? Should I open my office door so that others can see us in here? How often does my wife experience an orgasm? What if my wife is feeling the same way as this young woman?*

With sweat beads forming on his brow, the pastor responded, "You seem like such a dear person and I want you to get the very best advice. My good friend, a member of this church, is a physician, and I know he deals with these types of questions. Let me set up an appointment for you. In the meantime, I'm available to counsel your husband and you together as well as your husband one on one."

* * *

Sex. For some, the topic is taboo. Others find it repulsive. Those willing to market and exploit it make millions. Did you know that most couples have as much trouble talking about their own funeral as they do talking about sex? That could be why the Christian Church has largely gone silent on the issue.

Some have bought into the myth that sex is only to be discussed between a husband and a wife, yet while sex is sacred and the marriage bed should be guarded, the topic of sex must be discussed if it's going to truly be honored and protected. God is not afraid of the topic of sex. Did you know that God has given us more instructions about sex than

He has about parenting? The Bible provides more instruction and guidance for how to make a baby than for how to take care of one! God has given us sex as a gift and it's one to be thoroughly treasured, celebrated and enjoyed.

After being in relationship ministry 45 years, I have been asked by many people, "Gary, why have you never written a book on sex?" The answer is simple: "I don't know." I've talked about sex and the differences between men and women at my seminars and conferences, but I have never dedicated an entire book to one of God's greatest gifts to marriage: sex.

God has given us sex as a gift and it's one to be thoroughly treasured, celebrated and enjoyed.

That's why the book in your hands is so valuable. It's designed not only to strengthen your marriage and your relationship with your spouse, but also to equip you to have the best sex of your life. You're going to learn what it takes to raise the temperature in your relationship and create an atmosphere for sex. Then we're going to teach you how to celebrate the differences between you and your spouse. We're going to get into the nitty-gritty of sex—exploring foreplay, intercourse and cultivating creativity in your marriage. You're going to discover the spiritual dimensions of sex—something you may have never considered before. Finally, you'll get some keys on how to resolve conflict and guard your relationship so that you can enjoy the best sex of your life from this day forward.

Along the way, you'll discover tools to help you brush up your communication skills and find answers to some of the toughest questions on sex, romance and intimacy.

The majority of sexual issues in marriage can be traced back to relational struggles. This book is not designed to solve medical or psychological conditions in dealing with sex. We are not medical doctors or psychologists. We want to help you with the relational aspects of sex.

Keep in mind that we will not only be sharing general information that will be applicable for both the husband and wife; we'll also be giving very specific proven methods for each mate.

The Formula for Great Sex

Now you may be wondering, *How can Gary and Ted promise that I'm going to have the very best sex of my life?* That's because God designed sex to be so much more than just intercourse. In the upcoming chapters, we're going to discuss not just foreplay, intercourse and the afterglow, but also what it really takes to develop a foundation and atmosphere in your marriage for the absolute best sex—the kind that you and your spouse were made for!

Before we go too far, we need to introduce you to a simple but powerful equation:

$$\text{Honor} \rightarrow \text{Security} \rightarrow \text{Intimacy} \rightarrow \textit{Sex}$$

So what does this equation have to do with the best sex of your life? In the upcoming chapters, you're going to discover how honor creates security. Security creates intimacy. And intimacy sets the stage for great sex. The truth is that you cannot have great sex without honor and an open spirit.

The journey to the best sex of your life—the kind that God designed for you and your spouse—begins on the road to your heart. You begin honoring your love when you begin working on your own heart. It's easy to fall into the trap of thinking that your spouse is the source of conflict in a marriage, but the truth is that our own hearts often determine the outcome of a relationship. The best sex of your life starts in your heart, not in your head or between your legs.

The Road Map to the Best Sex of Your Life

What we want to give you in this book is a road map toward the best, most secure and safest relationship possible. As your relationship's honor and security are built, your sex life will be better than you can imagine.

To start off, never try to improve your sex life in marriage. Instead, develop honor and security in your relationship and you'll discover how great sex is a by-product of your loving relationship. It's like making money: If you simply try harder each day to increase your income, you'll discover how elusive money really is. It's like the pot of gold at the end of the rainbow. Don't chase the gold; learn how to serve people in love with a great product that they genuinely need. Offer great customer service and watch how money just seems to keep coming in. Sex is the same. Build more honor and security, and the sexual satisfaction will naturally increase.

> *The journey to the best sex of your life—the kind that God designed for you and your spouse—begins on the road to your heart.*

I (Gary) saw my own sexual relationship with Norma take major leaps forward as soon as I increased my own perceived value of her. That's what "honor" means: treating someone like a treasured gift or something of great value.

A number of years ago, I returned from a two-week conference where I learned about the value of honoring others. I realized that I had been expecting Norma to "make me happy" in the sexual area. At this conference, I learned a life-changing principle: When we give up our life for others, we gain it back from God.

I went home not knowing what to expect. All I wanted to do was serve my wife because God was filling me up with Himself. After three weeks, Norma asked me why I hadn't pursued sex. I surprised myself—I hadn't even thought of it! I was focusing on serving God and giving Him a chance to meet all of my needs, and He was faithfully doing it.

I explained to her that I didn't want to place any expectations on her but just serve her the best I could. Then she said something I'll never forget: "I need it too, you know. I need to be held and I enjoy it, too."

I had never heard those words before. When you dedicate yourself to serving, valuing and honoring your spouse, he or she will start looking for ways to love you back. My wife never resisted sex again.

In the next chapter, we're going to introduce you to the knowledge and skills you'll need to develop the best possible foundation for sex.

From GarySmalley.com

We receive emails each week at our GarySmalley.com website from people asking questions about their struggling marriages. We do our best to answer these questions with biblical truth and practical insight. This typical question from a woman who doesn't understand how sex is connected to sexual intimacy may sound familiar.

Q: *I have been married for 34 years, and during that time sex has always been an issue. For years I worked to please my husband—whatever it took, as often as he wanted—but at some point I simply became worn out. I did not know how to express my own needs in ways that he could hear, so they went unmet. At the moment we're merely enduring sex—it is not creating true intimacy for either of us. It feels forced and performance-based. I'm sick of it. Where do I start in resolving the sex script in my marriage?*

A: We want to applaud you for wanting to resolve this issue in your marriage. Most men are turned on sexually by what they see. Most women are turned on sexually by what they feel. Intimacy is about working at meeting the needs of your spouse. I truly believe a win-win is possible! You and your husband can bring safety to this area of your marriage. It sounds like you both desire a sense of security.

First, remember that *the only person you can change is yourself.* You cannot change your husband. This issue is not going to be solved in the bedroom. Start with the resolution that you are not going to change his sex drive or his goals for sex.

Second, *the issue is rarely the issue.* Ask yourself if sex is the real issue. Maybe your husband does not feel validated as a lover. Does he feel adequate? Sex is always an indicator reflecting the health of your marriage overall. Is he willing to find a win-win solution? If he is, start working on a solution you both can love. It may take a while, but it's worth the effort. Will he study this book with you? That would be the best for bringing up subjects to discuss, because it's a third party suggesting the discussions.

Sex will never satisfy you until you feel safe and your anger is being healed within you. Great sex requires an open spirit. Our spirits close after years of harsh words, emotional distance and frustration. Norma Smalley likes to use the "spirit tube" as a word picture for an open or closed spirit:

God did such a great job in creating us! If my tube is filled with rocks, I will not enjoy sex. I think God did that so we would not keep anger in our hearts. In the process of seeking forgiveness, I think it's important for the man to understand the importance of taking each rock out one at a time. Many men want to empty the tube all at once. That does not work. The rocks have been deposited over the years, and they take time to come back out.

It's also helpful for couples to have an anti-poison word contract, ideally exchanged at the altar. Norma and I promised each other that we would never use the word "hate" or say things like "I am going to divorce you" or "I can't stand you." Some words are so filled with poison that even when you ask forgiveness, it's hard to get them out of your mind.

If repeating yourself does not work, try something new. Consider counseling. Try telling him you deeply love him and want to spend the rest of your life with him, and this is an area you want to work on together. Ask him if he's willing to help find a solution that's win-win.

Intimacy does not start in the bedroom; it *culminates* in the bedroom. Sexual problems are indicative of greater issues. Focus on personal responsibility, and the road will be paved for safety and great communication—and hopefully the best sex of your life!

Summary

God has given us sex as a gift and it's one to be thoroughly treasured, celebrated and enjoyed.

The majority of sexual issues in marriage can be traced back to relational struggles.

God designed sex to be so much more than intercourse.

The great sex God designed for you and your spouse begins on the road to your heart.

Pillow Talk

How often, if ever, did you and your parents talk about sex?

What kind of picture did your parents paint for you of sex?

Are there any questions about sex that you think are off limits for us to discuss? If so, what are they?

On a scale of 1 to 10, 1 being stale and 10 being hot, how would you rate our marriage?

When do you feel loved the most by me?

CHAPTER 2

Raising the Temperature

Far too many couples approach sex hesitantly. I'm reminded of a story I used to tell at my seminars of a woman who went to a marriage conference. Her husband refused to go. She enjoyed the event and was so excited about everything she learned. When she returned home, she said, "Honey, I wish you could have been there—it was amazing! There's so much I want to share with you."

"That's great, but I've got a lot of things to get done right now. Let's go over it later," the husband responded.

"But could we just go over one of the things I learned? It's simple but powerful. Pretty please?" she begged.

"Okay—one thing, as long as it's quick," he responded.

"The speaker said that as your kids are growing up, it's important for you to do things together regularly as a couple. If we do a hobby or activity together now, then we won't have the empty-nest syndrome when our kids head off to college."

"You can't believe everything you hear at a seminar," the husband responded.

"But I really think it's true," the wife piped back. "In fact, I'm so fired up about this, I already know what we should do together."

The husband braced himself for what she was going to say next. "Will you teach me to hunt so we can go together?"

The husband couldn't believe it—his wife wanted to go hunting with him! Maybe these marriage seminars weren't so bad after all.

On her next birthday, he bought his wife a rifle. She was thrilled. The opening day of deer season they went out hunting. Somewhere in the forest, they separated. When the husband heard three shots fired in a row, he ran toward the direction of the shots. That's when he discovered his wife and a stranger yelling at each other. As he approached them, he heard the stranger say to his wife, "Fine—you can have your deer. Just let me get my saddle off it first!"

* * *

In many ways, all of us who are married or want to get married someday can relate to that woman: Half the time, we don't really know what we're shooting at when it comes to sex. We know we need knowledge and skills, but sometimes things don't turn out like we expect. And sometimes our biggest lessons come out of our biggest mistakes.

It all goes back to that equation we introduced in the first chapter:

HONOR ➝ Security ➝ Intimacy ➝ *Sex*

It took me (Gary) longer than I could have imagined to discover the truth of this equation. Yet it rings true in countless marriages. I have asked more than 10,000 couples worldwide the following questions:

- What do you think are the key things that strengthen a marriage relationship?

- What do you think are the key things that weaken a marriage relationship?

After interviewing countless couples, I realized that sex was somehow connected to the quality of the relationship—but it would take me many more years to figure out it all begins with honor. Over the years, I have learned a lot about how crucial honor is to a healthy marriage. My best instructor on this issue just happens to be my best friend—my wife, Norma.

Learning the Importance of Honor

When Norma and I first met, we dated on and off. We would regularly break up and get back together for the first four years we knew each other. We finally got married. (I still think it's amazing that she was willing to marry me.)

Shortly after the honeymoon, I began imitating the behavior of my dad without even realizing it. I was the last of six kids, and growing up, I watched my father explode in anger at my older brothers and sisters. My mother and father had many escalated arguments during my growing-up years. I learned quickly that as the youngest child, there are certain things you just don't say to your dad. It's better to stifle them.

I remember my dad throwing his dinner napkin on the table on more than one occasion and announcing angrily, "I'm out of here. There is no respect for me in this family!" To which my siblings would agree, "Great, get out of here!" So I grew up without knowing anything about a healthy family, let alone a healthy marriage. I never saw my dad hold my mom. I never knew what really loving someone meant. My older sisters tell me that my dad was a good-natured man and a jokester at times, but by the time I came on the scene, he must have been worn out by the first five kids.

I never knew how my childhood experiences would affect my relationship with Norma. I didn't realize that the way our parents model (or don't model) a relationship wreaks havoc in our lives for years to come. For the first five years, our marriage rapidly deteriorated, and I didn't know how to stop it. I would share with her specific things I thought she could do to improve our relationship.

One day I came home from work and Norma wasn't speaking to me. On this particular day, she didn't even turn to say "Hi" when I came in. I knew I was in hot water.

"What's wrong?" I asked shyly.

"Nothing!" she said firmly.

At the time, I didn't understand that communication—especially between a husband and wife—is mainly nonverbal. So "nothing" really meant "something."

"Can we talk about this?" I pressed.

She shook her head. A few hours later, she shared the brutal truth: The reason she never liked talking to me about the frustrations and hurts in our marriage was because I refused to change. I never made any adjustments. Talking about our issues had become too painful over the years. On that fateful day, I stopped and asked her what was wrong with our marriage. I had run out of ideas and was finally ready to listen to hers. I still remember Norma's words, "I've told you it a hundred times and it doesn't make sense to you."

"Please, tell me one more time. Norma, please," I begged.

She began to talk. For the first time in as long as I could remember, I listened to her every word, her every idea. That's when she said something that changed our marriage forever: "I feel like everything on this earth is more important to you than I am."

"Wait a minute! What do you mean that everything is more important on this earth than you are to me?" I asked, unsure what she was trying to get at.

"Just look—everything is more important to you," she responded. "Your work is more important. Your hunting and fishing are more important to you than I am. Everything is more important."

"Do you mean like the TV and stuff like that?" I asked.

"Yeah . . . TV and stuff like that."

The way I was living my life
communicated that almost anything
and everything were more important
than the person I loved.

I stared at her dumbfounded. I must have looked like one of those cartoon characters who had just been hit over the head with a frying pan. Of course, I didn't think television was more important than my wife. I wouldn't say that out loud in a million years. But my actions and attitudes were saying something else. The way I was living my life communicated that almost anything and everything were more important than the person I loved.

I made a decision that day that changed our marriage forever. I said, "I don't know how I am going to do this, but I want you to know that for the rest of my life, I am going to do everything I can to communicate to you that you are number one in my life. Of all the people on this earth, there is no person that is going to be more important to me than you. There is no trout, no television show, nothing on this earth that is going to be more important to me than you."

> The two most important principles that keep a couple in love and in a mutually satisfying relationship:
>
> (1) Honor your spouse.
>
> (2) Keep your relationship secure.

I immediately started learning how to honor my wife and make her a priority. What I discovered is that the foundation of what my wife and every spouse needs can be summed up in one word: *honor*. The word "honor" means to attach high value to someone or something. When we honor something or someone, a feeling often wells up inside of us and affects our actions and attitudes. For instance, if your favorite movie star came to your home for dinner, you would probably feel a little awestruck. You might think, *I am in the presence of someone really awesome.*

Yet the word "honor" hasn't just slipped away from our marriages—it's slipped away from our behavior and interactions. There is a lot of dishonor in our world. Rather than celebrating life and people, both are increasingly criticized and put down. The word "diss" (short for *dishonor* or *disrespect*) has even become popular. When we don't honor life—including our own—our attitudes begin to be affected.

Are you ever tempted to say things to yourself like, *I am an idiot, I'll never amount to anything* or *No one likes me*? Those statements are a reflection of the lack of honor we give ourselves. Each comment eats away at our emotions, our esteem and eventually our self-worth. Those kinds of comments don't just dishonor ourselves; they also dishonor the God who created us. Before we realize it, we are dishonoring those around us. The comments we make to ourselves become the comments we make to other people, and before we know it, we can provoke other people to treat us the way we truly feel about ourselves.

The comments we make to ourselves become the comments we make to other people.

The good news is that the opposite is also true! When we realize how valuable we are as people, our feelings for ourselves change. We begin changing the way we react and respond to other people and before we know it, people change the way they treat us.

Honoring Your Marriage

Honoring your spouse means honoring your marriage and the commitment you made on your wedding day. Did you know that marriage was not an institution designed by humans? Marriage finds its origin in God. Just like God created sex, which we'll discuss in greater detail in chapter 7, God created marriage for us as a gift.

In the beginning, God created humankind in His image and likeness: "Let us make man in our image, in our likeness" (Gen. 1:26). This doesn't refer to a physical likeness of God as much as it does the emotional and relational attributes of God.

Genesis 2:18 begins, "The LORD God said, 'It is not good for the man to be alone.'" In other words, man is better off when someone is with him. So God said, "I will make a helper suitable for him." The word "helper" implies that the man needs someone to come alongside him where he is lacking. The Hebrew word for "helper" in Genesis 2:18 is *ezer*, which means "one who helps." It refers to someone who comes alongside to offer assistance. In fact, it is the same word that is used in Psalms 33, 70 and 115 to refer to God. He is your helper in times of trouble, your helper in times of difficulty:

We wait in hope for the LORD; he is our *help* and our shield (Ps. 33:20, emphasis added).

Hasten, O God, to save me; O LORD, come quickly to *help* me (Ps. 70:1, emphasis added).

O house of Israel, trust in the LORD—he is their *help* and shield (Ps. 115:9, emphasis added).

God gave you a spouse to come alongside you to give you assistance. He did not give you a spouse as a replacement for Himself. He meets your needs, and you are 100-percent responsible for your spiritual journey. There's a spiritual dimension to sex that we'll explore in chapter 10, but it's important to realize right now that your mate is zero-percent responsible for your spiritual journey. Ladies, you are zero-percent responsible for your husband's journey. Same goes for the guys. But we get to be *helpers*. We can offer love, honor, encouragement and support. You are the CEO of your life; your spouse is not. You are responsible to God for how you live your life.

After God decided that it was not good for man to be alone, it says in Genesis that He caused the man to fall into a deep sleep. While he was sleeping, God took out one of the man's ribs and closed up the place with flesh. Then God made a woman from the rib He had taken out of the man. Genesis 2:23 says, "The man said, 'this is now bone of bones and flesh of my flesh; she shall be called "woman," for she was taken out of man.'" Adam now had a spiritual, emotional and physical companion.

God's plan for your marriage is that you spend your entire lifetime learning and growing together.

This was the first marriage. You see, God's plan for your marriage is that you spend your entire lifetime learning and growing together.

Maybe that's one reason why the Bible says in the book of Malachi that God hates divorce (see Mal. 2:16). It's not the divorced person that God hates but the breaking of the bonds that naturally happen in marriage. While those who have gone through a divorce can experience grace, freedom, forgiveness and restoration from the Lord, divorce is against God's best plan for your life.

You may be tempted to consider divorce as an option. You or someone you know may be ready to give up on their marriage. But God can work miracles in all relationships. You don't have to give in. You can begin fighting for your marriage today!

I (Ted) made this decision a few years into my marriage. Amy and I were vacationing at Jekyll Island off the shore of Georgia. I remember looking at her and making a commitment: "Amy, I will be honest with you. For the first seven years of ministry and our marriage, I wanted to be known. I wanted to be known as a great leader, speaker and teacher. My priorities have been off. When I die, I want to be known for two things: I want to be known as a great husband and I want to be known as a great father. So no matter how good or bad things get, know that you're stuck with me forever."

Amy didn't say a word. She didn't need to—the joy on her face was unforgettable.

When we verbally remind our spouses that we're committed no matter what, we don't just honor our marriages, we also honor our spouses. Secure in that love, the relationship can't help but blossom and grow.

Honoring Your Love Every Day

Our attitudes and emotions grow out of the word "honor." When was the last time you turned to your love and said, "Unbelievable! It's just unbelievable. I can't believe I am actually sitting next to you!" How did it feel to you? How do you think the other person felt? If you've never said something like this to your spouse, try it. You might feel a little uncomfortable at first—that's natural. But when you make such comments (and we encourage you to!), what you're really saying is that you can't believe that you are in the presence of someone very valuable—

you are honoring that person. You're saying, "You're valuable to me! You're significant! You're worthwhile! You matter!" The best part is that you can do this all the time. I (Gary) did this regularly, not just to my wife, but also to my children. My son would be watching TV and I would walk into the room and announce, "Unbelievable!"

Sometimes I got down on my knees and said, "I cannot believe that I am in the same house with you!"

He usually said "D-a-a-a-d" with a smile and a loving roll of the eyes. But I did it anyway—because I want my wife and kids to know how valuable they are to me.

Honoring Your Love with Scripture

Honoring the love of your life is simply recognizing your mate's incredible worth. One of the ways that I've learned to honor my wife is by using Scripture. I find passages and read my wife's name right into the Bible:

[Name of love] was not a mistake, for all her days are written in Your book (see Ps. 139:15-16).

How precious are your thoughts about [name of love], O God. They cannot be numbered! I can't even count them; they outnumber the grains of sand! (Ps. 139:17-18, *NLT*).

You are [name of love]'s Father, and You love [him/her] even as You love Your Son, Jesus (see John 17:23).

You chose [name of love] when You planned creation (see Eph. 1:11-12).

It is Your desire to lavish Your love on [name of love] (see 1 John 3:1).

Look for Scriptures that you can use to remind yourself how God sees the love of your life, and to honor and pray for your spouse!

Honoring Your Love with Confirmation Bias

Another way to honor your love is through a breakthrough concept called *confirmation bias*. Here's the secret: When you make a decision about someone, your feelings follow. People tend to only see what they believe, so if you believe your spouse is worthless, incompetent or always late, you will only see and recognize the behaviors that support those beliefs.

I (Ted) recently saw the movie *Sentinel,* which concerns the investigation of the murder of a Secret Service agent. The lead investigator for the Secret Service is David Breckinridge (played by Keifer Sutherland of *24* fame), who is surprised when the city police have solved the case after just 30 minutes. "You know what I don't like about assumptions like that?" Breckinridge says. "You tend now to only look for the evidence that backs up what you believe and you won't see fresh or new evidence. You won't even be looking for it."

Too often, that's what we're tempted to do in our marriage. We make subconscious or even conscious decisions about our mate's behaviors, attitudes or even worth, and then we only look for evidence that backs up our conclusion.

*When you make a decision about
someone, your feelings follow.*

So if you believe your spouse is lazy, you will only see the behaviors that back up that belief. You may be overly critical when your spouse enjoys an hour of television, yet overlook the times your spouse bathes the children, washes the cars, mows the lawn or prepares dinner. You won't see those things, which is why the Scripture says, "Whatever is true, whatever is noble, whatever is right, whatever is pure, whatever is lovely, and whatever is admirable—if anything is excellent or praiseworthy—think about such things" (Phil. 4:8). Focus on those things. In fact, we encourage you to get a pen and a sheet of paper right now and make a list of the ways your spouse exemplifies each of these qualities.

Commit to prayerfully focusing on these attributes of your spouse for the next seven days. You'll be amazed at how your attitude and relationship will change! That's the secret of confirmation bias, and it bears repeating: When you make a decision about someone, your feelings follow. So go ahead and make the best possible decisions about your spouse!

Ellen's Happy Ending

Do you remember the story about Ellen that we began in chapter 1? Well, we're thrilled to report that Ellen's story has a happy ending—a very happy ending. And honor is at the heart of it.

Ellen was a member of a medium-sized church—not so small that everyone knew each person's business, but not so large that Ellen could hide in the crowd. It was just big enough so that she knew a lot of first names, but she didn't share her life with any of the people. And that's what made it hard for Ellen to approach her pastor with her frustration about sex: She only knew him on a surface level and had no idea how he would react.

Ellen's pastor honored her questions and frustrations. Her pastor even took her husband aside privately and drew him some pictures. He explained to him in very practical ways how he could pleasure his wife.

Ellen's husband, though he was shocked and completely embarrassed by the discussion and tutorial, worked through it. He honored her in a big way. First, he honored her by listening to her feelings and understanding her concerns. Later that same week, he honored her by blessing her with her first orgasm of their married life.

The next week, Ellen's husband thanked the pastor profusely. Honor was where it all started for Ellen: a pastor who listened, and a husband who loved. They worked through their issues and connected with each other like never before. And you and your spouse can, too! No matter what sexual issue you're struggling with, this book is going to help you more than you can imagine. In the next chapter, you'll discover how to create an atmosphere for the best sex of your life.

From GarySmalley.com

Q: *I married my Prince Charming but fear the happily-ever-after is not going to happen. Was it really love, or did I get caught up in the fantasy and glamour of the whole thing?*

A: Sleeping Beauty, Cinderella and Snow White went through some tough times before they got their happily-ever-after, and guess what? Your marriage will go through them, too.

Most of us come into adulthood with a distorted vision of a healthy love relationship. Our models of love often come from songs, books, friends, movies and television, which depict love as fast-blooming, overwhelming, intense, romantic and requited. But these models display only one stage of love, the very first stage, which is heavily influenced by infatuation caused by chemistry. Good marriages contain many more elements than just chemistry, yet the lovers in our books and movies never get far enough into the story to see them. We don't know whether the lovers stayed together long enough to determine if they were committed for the long term. We see an hour and a half of two people enduring misunderstanding and frustration and then going romantically off into the sunset. We never get to see what happens next.

These images of love leave us with serious misconceptions, such as:

- Passion equals love.
- My lover should meet all my needs.
- Once love dies, you can't get it back.
- Chemistry is all that matters.
- Love conquers all.
- When things get tough, it means you have the wrong partner.
- My lover should make me happy.
- Once in love, you stay on a high forever.
- Love is a feeling, and you either have it or you don't.

These are all lies or, at best, gross misunderstandings of the true nature of love. Chemistry plays itself out. You eventually come off the high of infatuation. But that does not mean that love is dead. Not at all. In fact, it may be just beginning.

Now the work begins. All the behavioral skills in the world won't pump life back into an ailing marriage if the couple doesn't trust each other, if they don't feel safe, unconditionally loved, valued and understood. Are you creating a safe and secure marriage?

All marriages go through ups and downs. You are not experiencing anything that we all haven't felt a time or two. The key is to listen to your feelings but not rest on them for decisions. Love is not sustained on feelings alone. The decision to honor and love is where you rest your marriage.

Instead of waiting for a fairy-tale ending to just show up, start creating your own happily-ever-after. Great endings do not just happen. They take a lot of hard work. That hard work is played out over many years.

You are only in the first 100 yards of a marathon. Keep running!

Summary

The two most important principles that keep a couple in a mutually satisfying relationship are: (1) Honor your spouse, and (2) keep your relationship secure.

Honor is esteeming your mate as highly valuable.

Honoring your spouse means honoring your marriage and the commitment you made on your wedding day.

The comments we make to ourselves become the comments we make to other people.

When we realize how valuable we are as people, our feelings for ourselves change.

Our attitudes and emotions grow out of honor.

When you make a decision about someone, your feelings follow.

Pillow Talk

What do you think are the key things that strengthen a marriage relationship?

What do you think are the key things that weaken a marriage relationship?

Are you ever tempted to say things to yourself like, *I am an idiot* or *I'll never amount to anything* or *No one likes me*?

CHAPTER 3

Creating the Atmosphere

One late night, Amy and I (Ted) were in bed reading together. She was enjoying a book by Shaunti Feldhahn called *For Women Only*. The book informs women of the tendencies of the male brain. As she was reading, she looked at me mid-page and asked a firecracker of a question: "Do you struggle with lusting after other women?"

"Yes, I do," I answered without missing a beat.

"That makes me so mad," she said.

"At who? Me or God?" I asked.

"What's God have to do with this?" she retorted.

"For some reason, God designed the male brain to be turned on visually," I answered.

Then there was silence. It was a little touch and go for the next few minutes, but that one question opened the door for us to talk, share and pray. Then Amy said something I'll never forget: "I want you to know that I am going to do everything in my power to help you not struggle with that anymore."

My response was simply, "Boom-boom-chicky-chicky-boom-boom!" And I thought, *I'm loving this book even more tonight—you just keep on going!*

At the core of the conversation, we weren't really talking about sex or even temptation. We were really talking about deeper heart issues: desires. A lot of people consider sex a need, but the truth is that sex is a desire. Air, food and water—those are needs, but you can go without sex and still live.

I decided to turn the question back on Amy and ask her about her desires. She shared that she would love for me to be at home every day by 4 P.M., so she could go running while I watched the kids. Knowing that's her personal desire, I try to make it my goal every day. There are some days I miss out on providing this for her, but she knows I make every effort to be home for her.

> *A lot of people consider sex a need, but the truth is that sex is a desire.*

That night I discovered something that changed our relationship forever—we both want to feel secure in our marriage. And one of the best ways to build security is to pour your energy into honoring your spouse and looking for opportunities to meet and nurture his or her desires. When you create security in your relationship, the temperature of your love life will go up.

Honor ➔ **SECURITY** ➔ Intimacy ➔ *Sex*

In this chapter, we're going to look at how you can create security in your marriage. We're going to explore how you can build a foundation for security in your relationship and cultivate security for years to come.

Discovering Your Spouse's Greatest Desires

Jesus said that "the greatest among you will be your servant" (Matt. 23:11). That means that if you truly love your mate, you'll work at discovering and meeting not just your spouse's basic needs, but also his or her desires. I believe this is so important that over the last few years, I have replaced the word "romance" with the word "security" in my conversations. Sometimes a couple will come to my office and say, "We have a sex problem."

My response: "You don't have a sex problem; you have an intimacy problem. You have an intimacy problem because you have a security problem. And you have a security problem because you have an honor problem."

Sex is only a barometer of the marriage. Honor leads to security, security leads to intimacy and intimacy leads to sex. Security means building honor into your relationship and esteeming your mate as highly valuable. Security means seeing your mate as personally autographed by God. When you grow the security within your marriage, the natural fruit is intimacy.

When I was 22, I married a beautiful, smart, feisty young woman named Amy Freitag. We recently celebrated our 11-year anniversary. I can honestly say that our love is stronger, our intimacy is deeper and our sex life is far better than it's ever been. In fact, Amy teases me that my testosterone level has gone up in the last three years. Do you want to know our secret? It's actually nothing new. In fact, it's tucked into one of the oldest books of the Bible: Song of Songs.

Song of Songs is one of the steamiest books of the Bible. Consider the first few verses:

Let him kiss me with the kisses of his mouth—for your love is more delightful than wine. Pleasing is the fragrance of your perfumes; your name is like perfume poured out. No wonder the maidens love you! Take me away with you—let us hurry! Let the king bring me into his chambers (Song of Songs 1:1-4).

You know what happens next! A modern translation of what Solomon's wife says in the first three verses might read, "Kiss me madly—your name is like a hot Krispy Kreme doughnut right off the conveyor belt." In other words, "The mere mention of your name evokes feelings in me. Your character is amazing to me."

The woman then says, "No wonder the maidens love you!" In other words, "I know other women want you. The mere mention of your name doesn't just entice me; others are enticed, but I am honored and blessed to get you." Then she urges, "Take me away with you—let us hurry!" This is every man's dream come true! She's saying, "I want you. I want you alone. I want to be with you alone." Notice that she's not talking

The Five Levels of Sexual Intimacy

LEVEL 1

IDENTIFICATION: Eye to body, eye to eye

EXPLANATION: Attraction and desire

SCRIPTURE: "Dark am I, yet lovely, O daughters of Jerusalem, dark like the tents of Kedar, like the tent curtains of Solomon. Do not stare at me because I am dark, because I am darkened by the sun. My mother's sons were angry with me and made me take care of the vineyards; my own vineyard I have neglected" (Song of Songs 1:5-6).

"I liken you, my darling, to a mare harnessed to one of the chariots of Pharaoh" (Song of Songs 1:9).

LEVEL 2

IDENTIFICATION: Hand to hand, hand to shoulder, hand to waist, hand to face, hand to head

EXPLANATION: Delay

SCRIPTURE: "My lover is to me a sachet of myrrh resting between my breasts" (Song of Songs 1:13).

"His left arm is under my head, and his right arm embraces me" (Song of Songs 2:6).

"My dove in the clefts of the rock, in the hiding places on the mountainside, show me your face, let me hear your voice; for your voice is sweet, and your face is lovely" (Song of Songs 2:14).

LEVEL 3

IDENTIFICATION: Mouth to face, mouth to mouth, mouth to body

EXPLANATION: Intimate touch

SCRIPTURE: "Until the day breaks and the shadows flee, turn, my lover, and be like a gazelle or like a young stag on the rugged hills" (Song of Songs 2:17).

"Your lips drop sweetness as the honeycomb, my bride; milk and honey are under your tongue. The fragrance of your garments is like that of Lebanon" (Song of Songs 4:11).

LEVEL 4

IDENTIFICATION: Body to body

EXPLANATION: Intercourse

SCRIPTURE: "Awake, north wind, and come, south wind! Blow on my garden, that its fragrance may spread abroad. Let my lover come into his garden and taste its choice fruits" (Song of Songs 4:16).

"I have come into my garden, my sister, my bride; I have gathered my myrrh with my spice. I have eaten my honeycomb and my honey; I have drunk my wine and my milk. *Eat, O friends, and drink; drink your fill, O lovers*" (Song of Songs 5:1, emphasis added because the last part of the verse is God speaking directly to the couple).

LEVEL 5*

IDENTIFICATION: The Real Climax

EXPLANATION: Commitment and depth

SCRIPTURE: "Place me like a seal over your heart, like a seal on your arm; for love is as strong as death, its jealousy unyielding as the grave. It burns like blazing fire, like a mighty flame. Many waters cannot quench love; rivers cannot wash it away. If one were to give all the wealth of his house for love, it would be utterly scorned" (Song of Songs 8:6-7).

How's that for an unquenchable sex life! The best sex of your life is on the road of faithfulness and commitment.

*Note: Most couples never reach Level 5 on this chart. That's because great sex is at the end of the road of resolved conflict. The open spirit is the key ingredient. When couples stop at Level 4, they get less than half of what God really designed sex to be. The best sex is a reflection of commitment and depth.

about physical features yet; she begins by focusing on that which cannot be seen.

Now stop and think for a moment:
When your love mentions your name, what
immediately comes to mind about you?

The Song of Songs oozes with this kind of language, which raises the question, *What kind of man was Solomon that women wanted him so much?* The answer? *He was a man who knew how to honor and create security for women.*

Building a Foundation of Security Before Marriage

So how do you build a healthy foundation for a great marriage and sex life? There are three ways to build a healthy foundation of security in your marriage. Here are three critically important steps to take *before* you are married.

1. Make Sure Your Character Runs Ahead of Your Desire

While it's good to ask someone, "Are you a Christian?" before you begin dating, it's better to ask, "Are you a follower of Jesus?" The two questions may sound the same, but there's a huge difference between them. A person who says, "I'm a Christian," may say so because he or she was confirmed at 12 years of age or grew up in a Christian home. But a person who says, "I'm a follower of Jesus," suggests that he or she reads the Bible, prays regularly and has a growing relationship with God. If a person just says he or she is a Christian, you can make a lot of assumptions that may or may not be true.

Before you begin dating, find out about the person's character. Remember that character will manifest itself in self-control. How does the person respond to frustration? Disappointment? Does the person treat you with respect—verbally, spiritually and physically? Does the person know his or her own boundaries?

2. Avoid Shortcuts

Solomon advises, "Do not arouse or awaken love until it so desires" (Song of Songs 3:5), and I believe this is one of his most brilliant pieces of wisdom.

I (Ted) often ask young men, "Do you want to be known as a stud?" The guys usually cheer. Then I encourage them to practice abstinence. I remind them that one day they may be with a young lady who was abused by her father or another family member. The only type of love she knows is physical. I tell them, "You'll be the first man in her life to stand up and say, 'No, we are not going to do it. I am not going to show you love physically before I cultivate security in marriage. We are going to do this the right way.'" That's a true stud.

3. Don't Rush Marriage

I never encourage anyone to rush into marriage just to have sex. That is one of the worst things you can do. If you don't cultivate the five areas that constitute a healthy relationship—character, curiosity and fascination, connection, good conflict resolution, and commitment—you'll only be running toward an unhealthy relationship. We have been through that rodeo way too many times in our counseling office, and it doesn't work. Men need to show restraint and self-control, and if your love can't do that, it's time to move on to someone else who has character. Marriage is a valid solution to the desire to have sex (see 1 Cor. 7). However, Paul is not validating a rushed marriage.

If you're a guy and you struggle with sexual lust and temptation, then chapter 12 will help you win the battle with lust once and for all. If you want to go deeper into this topic, I (Gary) encourage you to pick up a copy of *Change Your Heart, Change Your Life: How Changing What You Believe Will Give You the Life You've Always Wanted*. In chapter 5, I share a personal story of how I found power and freedom in this area of my life.

Growing Security Within Marriage

Once you've built a foundation for security in your marriage, you can continue to grow security for years to come. But even if you're just beginning today, there are several ways to cultivate security in your relationship.

1. Guard Your Spouse's Heart

My greatest desire as I love my wife and lay down my life for her is that her heart will stay open to me. In Song of Songs 2:15, Solomon's girlfriend says, "Catch for us the foxes." While that can be interpreted many ways, I think it points to the "foxes" of conflict that run through all of our lives. In essence, she's saying, "When conflict arises let's take care of it right away." When you take care of the "foxes," you create security, and intimacy naturally grows.

2. Create Boundaries

One of the best things Amy and I did when we got married was to move 1,000 miles away from our families. That may sound harsh, but we were able to work through things together without having any sort of meddling going on.

Adam and Eve did not have a biological father and mother, so Genesis 2:24—"For this reason a man will leave his father and mother"—was written in the future tense, for those coming after Adam and Eve. The verse also reveals that there will be roadblocks that stand in the way of healthy unity or oneness.

Far too many couples come into the office struggling because their parents are meddling in the relationship. While it's important to spend time with family members, these relationships should be healthy.

My own in-laws have been great examples of what a healthy relationship with family members looks like. Amy and her mom, Linda, are very close friends, but I can say that in 10-plus years of marriage, I have never once felt Linda meddling in our marriage. Linda is very much rooted in Scripture. She knows that it is God-ordained for a couple to leave their own families and cleave to each other.

Ephesians 5:31 says, "For this cause shall a man leave his father and mother, and shall cleave to his wife; and the two shall become one flesh" (*ASV*). That word for "cleave" is translated as "glue" in modern Hebrew. A married man and woman are designed to become glue, but that natural bond cannot form if they are still cleaving to Mom and Dad. And that glue will have a hard time bonding if they are cleaving to friends, old dating relationships or other addictions.

I love it when a mom comes up to me at a wedding and says, "I don't feel like I am losing a daughter today—I feel like I'm gaining a son." My response is simple and blunt: "Nope! You are losing a daughter." That perspective—that one must *leave* in order to *cleave*—is the key to launching a young couple into oneness in marriage.

3. Don't Use Sex as a Weapon or Reward

Sex is beautiful and wonderful. It is also very powerful. Sex is not meant to be used as a weapon or a reward. Rather, it's meant to be mutually enjoyed in a safe environment. The best sex of your life requires communication. Now there will be more than a few moments in a marriage when it's not the optimal time for sex. It's okay to say, "Not right now" or "I need some time," but remember the scriptural guidance on this. The Bible instructs that a married couple should "not deprive each other [of sex] except by mutual consent and for a [limited] time" (1 Cor. 7:5). Sex should never be used to manipulate or control the person you love.

4. Commit Sexually to Your Spouse for Life

When the Bible says that the two "will become one flesh," it means that the man and woman are united (Gen. 2:24). While this literally means a physical consummation of the marriage, it also suggests that a couple is super-glued together on all levels. They become one. Before the Fall, the man and his wife were both naked (or as my pastor as I was growing up would say, "neck-ed") and they felt no shame (see Gen. 2:25). Not only were they physically naked, they had also never been exposed to sin. They were perfectly united; they had oneness.

5. Enjoy Make-up Sex by Practicing the Five-Minute Rule

I've learned that the Five-Minute Rule can go a long way in protecting the bonds of love, respect and security in a marriage. Basically, this rule means that when a conflict happens, take a five-minute time-out. Let me tell you how this rule came about.

In the past, whenever Amy and I would get into a disagreement, I would shut down emotionally. I would close my heart; I'd actually hide out in the basement and wait for her to come to apologize. Our conversations went something like this:

"Ted, I'm sorry."

"That's good," I replied, playing it cool.

"I shouldn't have said those things," she graciously said.

I thought it was her responsibility to keep my heart open. I thought if she said the right things and I reacted well to them, then my heart would be open before her and God. Boy was I wrong! I didn't even realize that I was offering her conditional love. In essence, I was making my love for her performance-based.

But the Bible challenges us in our relationships to "be completely humble and gentle . . . bearing with one another in love" (Eph. 4:2). I have learned that it's not Amy's responsibility to keep my heart open—it's my own.

So I started using the Five-Minute Rule. In essence, I put myself in a time-out. Following the instruction of James 1:19—"Be quick to listen, slow to speak and slow to become angry"—I go away for at least five minutes and ask God to help me open my heart back up. During this time, I refuse to sulk, pout, whine, complain or even come up with three reasons why it's her fault. I take 100-percent responsibility for my heart. And every time I do, the bond of our love, respect and security is not only preserved but also nurtured.

The Five-Minute Rule has helped our hearts stay open to each other. And when the heart is open, every door opens: to great conversations, time together, intimacy and sex.

If you have never had make-up sex with your mate, learn to resolve conflict before your head hits the pillow. It can make for a great time once the sun is down (chapter 11 is an entire chapter on conflict and make-up sex).

In the next chapter, you'll discover why men and women are so different—and how you can begin celebrating those differences in your own marriage.

From GarySmalley.com

Q: *Dating was great. Our marriage is not so great. What happened to the love and excitement we once had?*

A: Dating is all about curiosity and fascination. We spend countless hours getting to know the one we love. We ask great questions, diving deep into the heart of another. In the Song of Songs, King Solomon paints a wonderful word picture of this stage of love:

> My dove in the clefts of the rock, in the hiding places on the mountainside, show me your face, let me hear your voice; for your voice is sweet, and your face is lovely (Song of Songs 2:14).

Solomon is saying, "I want to get to know you." He loves it when she speaks and shares herself with him. He wants to communicate with her.

Marriage brings new components: *duty* and *responsibility*. When you are dating, you don't share bills, household chores and child-rearing.

The key is not to *replace* curiosity and fascination with duty and responsibility. We must balance them all. My wife did not fall in love with me because of my job or the fact that I was great at mowing the lawn, but because I got to know her. She felt what Solomon's beloved felt: "My lover is mine and I am his" (Song of Songs 2:16).

Continue to ask each other great questions to get to know each other deeply. Keep a regular date night, free from distraction. Revisit some of the places you frequented on your first dates. If they are too far away, reminisce about your favorite restaurants, past vacations, honeymoon spot, and so on.

After 40 years of marriage, I am still finding out new nuggets about Norma. I am very fascinated by her!

Never stop asking questions. Never stop mining for nuggets in your love's heart.

Norma and I love eating at Joe's Crab Shack in our hometown of Branson, Missouri. We usually end our night out with a brisk walk along beautiful Lake Taneycomo. You would think that after 40 years of marriage there was nothing more to learn about the person you married. Not true! Though I know how Norma will respond to just about every situation, she still surprises me.

One Thursday night, we finished up our lobster bisque at Joe's and headed for our walking path when Norma's knee hurt and became very weak. I thought for sure she would want me to help her back to the car. Wrong! She looked down at her knee and said, "I'm going to walk tonight, and if I have to, I am going to drag you along behind me." I was shocked.

It saddens me to think of a couple who live together but are no longer fascinated by the actions and life of each other. I'm blessed to get to spend a lifetime as a student of my mate.

Live in fascination, wonder and awe of your mate. Watch what that does for security!

Summary

Many people consider sex a need, but the truth
is that sex is a desire. Air, food and water are needs.
Without them, you die.

Develop your character in Christ for self-control in sex.

Creating security in marriage requires you to create
healthy boundaries with family and friends.

Sex should never be used to manipulate,
control or reward your mate.

Pillow Talk

When you hear my name, what immediately
comes to your mind?

To become a fully devoted follower of
Jesus Christ, I want to . . .

Do you think we have healthy boundaries
with our family? What could we do to strengthen
our bond in this marriage?

CHAPTER 4

Celebrate Differences

One of my (Gary's) friends is a massive guy who plays professional football. He once shared with me a story from his honeymoon that I've never forgotten.

By the evening of his wedding day, he and wife were already at odds. It had only been a few hours since the wedding ceremony and the young couple was already tripping over the differences between them.

My friend decided to take control of the relationship and establish who the real leader was. He grabbed a pair of his pants out of the suitcase, threw them toward his wife and said, "Honey, put those on."

His petite wife picked them up, looked at them and said, "These are huge! I can't put these on. They're too big."

"That's right!" he said. "And I want to establish right now who wears the pants in our home."

The wife reached into her suitcase, pulled out a dainty pair of pink lace panties and shot them at him like a rubber band.

"Try those on," she countered.

"I can't get into those," the husband responded.

"You're right!" she answered. "And you'll never get into them again unless you change your attitude."

* * *

Intimacy in a relationship begins by establishing honor and security, not by demanding respect. But it's hard to build honor and security without understanding the created differences between men and women.

That's why we want to look at the broad outlines of these differences, and then highlight the five key differences between men and women that increase honor and security if understood and practiced, but weaken the relationship if ignored or violated.

True Intimacy

Discovering true intimacy begins with understanding the unique differences between men and women—God-created differences between men and women. It does not begin in the bedroom. Intimacy begins with honor and security as we explored in the last chapters, and it results in sex, as we'll discover in the next chapter.

Honor ➤ Security ➤ **INTIMACY** ➤ *Sex*

Intimacy includes the everyday acts of kindness, consistency and communication that build longing and eventually create a desire for sex in women. The best sex of your life begins with what some might consider nonsexual contact—holding hands, touching shoulders, a warm hug.

The differences between men and women when it comes to sex are striking. The average man is ready for the sexual union in a matter of seconds. But the average woman takes much longer—in some cases hours or even days of being treated like a valuable person—to emotionally desire to share physical intimacy with her husband. Many men don't realize it, but more than 80 percent of a woman's need for meaningful touch is nonsexual. The best sex of your life begins with honoring and celebrating these differences.

Brain Sex

In their bestselling book, *Brain Sex: The Real Difference Between Men and Women*, Anne Moir and David Jessel write that a hundred years ago, the observation that men were different from women in a whole range of aptitudes, skills and abilities would have been considered yawningly obvious, but such a remark uttered today evokes very different reactions. If said by a man, it might suggest a certain social ineptitude, a naïveté in matters of sexual politics, a sad deficiency in conventional wisdom or a clumsy attempt to be provocative. If said by a woman, it might be seen as a betrayal of the hard-fought victories of recent decades as women have sought equality of status, opportunity and respect.

The authors observe, "Yet the truth is that virtually every professional scientist and researcher into the subject has concluded that the brains of men and women are different. There has seldom been a greater divide between what intelligent, enlightened opinion presumes—that men and women have the same brain—and what science knows—that they do not."[1]

There are some good reasons to be educated on gender differences:

- To honor differences
- To increase curiosity and fascination
- To meet the desires of your mate
- To better offer understanding and forgiveness
- To discover an antidote for negative beliefs and assumptions

The authors of *Brain Sex* believe the inherent differences between men and women begin in the brain. They write:

> The brain, the chief administrative and emotional organ of life, is differently constructed in men and in women; it processes information in a different way, which results in different perceptions, priorities and behaviour. In the past ten years there has been an explosion of scientific research into what makes the sexes different. Doctors, scientists, psychologists and sociologists, working apart, have produced a body of findings which, taken together, paints a remarkably consistent picture. And the picture is one of startling sexual asymmetry.[2]

Trait	Women	Men
Chromosomes	XX	XY
Blood volume	4/5 of a gallon	1.5 gallons
Muscle mass	20% of body weight	40% of body weight
Side of brain favored	Bilateral, but right dominant	Left dominant
Sexual thoughts	Once a day, 3 to 4 on really "hot" days	33 times by noon
Words per minute	250	125
Eye-contact skills	Study faces and people	Study things and environment
Eye-contact development	Skills of baby girls increase 400% in first 3 months of life	Skills of baby boys increase 0% in first 3 months of life
Social skills	In games, girls take turns 20 times more often than boys	Boys are 20 times more aggressive than girls
Core fears	Disconnection and abandonment	Being controlled and failure
Communication style	Express emotions	Express facts
Communication goal	Understanding	Solutions
Definition of intimacy	T-A-L-K	Sex
Relational style	Personal	Objective[3]

Did you know that every cell in a man's body is different from every cell in a woman's body? That makes *millions* of inherent differences. The chemicals flowing through our bodies are different. Our muscle structure is different. Even our immune systems are different! Because a woman has two X chromosomes, she actually has a stronger immune system than a man. Women are stronger than men at conception. Fewer baby girls die before and after birth. Women have fewer diseases and are better able to resist certain diseases.

Did you know that even the blood of men and women is different? Men have almost one million more red blood cells in every drop of

Right-brain Controls	Left-brain Controls
Visual	Verbal
Spatial	Linguistic
Big picture	Details
Emotional	Practical
Abstract	Concrete
Shapes and patterns	Orderly sequences[4]

blood than women do. In addition, men have an average of one-and-a-half gallons of blood flowing through their bodies, while women only have four-fifths of a gallon. Meanwhile, 40 percent of a man's body weight is muscle while only 20 percent of a woman's body weight is muscle. And men's skin is thicker and bones heavier. That's why on a daily basis, men can often outwork women in hard-labor jobs. That's also why men often win arm-wrestling matches with women.

Women have a lot of insulating cells throughout their body that make them more attractive. It also makes it easier for women to gain weight and harder for them to lose it. Those cells have come in handy historically for women during times of famine as well as during pregnancy.

Brainwashed?

One of the most fascinating things we discovered in our research about the differences between men and women is that for the first few days after conception, we all look the same. We all look like little girls—you can't tell that little boys are little boys. Then something miraculous happens: Mom releases a chemical that starts flowing through the body. If the embryo is a little girl, nothing happens, but if it's a little boy, the release of testosterone is stimulated. Testosterone changes our bodies, and it naturally drives us sexually and makes us more aggressive. Testosterone washes the little male brain.

The result is that men are lateral-brained. We use one side of the brain at a time. Meanwhile, women are bilateral in the brain. They use both sides. Women physically have more and larger connecting fibers between the two halves of their brain. That means women have greater access between the two sides, which contributes to intuition. That's why in any given moment, women can take in more information than men.

If we flashed up subliminal messages on a screen and asked a group of men and women to write them down, the women would write them down and the men would scurry to catch up with comments such as, "Did you see that?" and "I didn't catch that." Women are naturally alert. They hear and see more at any given time because of the way their brains are wired.

Men tend to favor the left side of the brain. This is where the language system is stored. It's where we get logic, engineering and accounting. Women tend to favor the right side, which is creative.

Now what's really interesting is that this is not true for every man and every woman—it's only true about 80 percent of the time. So there are some women who are left-brain dominant and some men who are right-brain dominant, and you may be one of them! Want to find out if you are in the 80 percent or in the 20 percent? Take the Brain Sex Test to see which side of the brain you favor.

The Brain Sex Test

1. You hear an indistinct meow. Without looking around, how well can you place the location of the cat?

    (a) If you think about it you can point to it.
    (b) You can point straight to it.
    (c) You don't know if you could point to it.

2. How good are you at remembering a song you've just heard?

    (a) You find it easy and you can sing part of it in tune.
    (b) You can only do it if it's simple and rhythmic.
    (c) You find it difficult.

3. A person you've met a few times telephones you. How easy is it for you to recognize his or her voice in the few seconds before the person tells you who they are?

    (a) You find it quite easy.
    (b) You recognize the voice at least half the time.
    (c) You recognize the voice less than half the time.

4. You're with a group of married friends, two of whom are having an affair. Would you detect their relationship?

    (a) Nearly always
    (b) Half the time
    (c) Seldom

5. You're at a large and purely social gathering. You're introduced to five strangers. If their names are mentioned the following day, how easy is it for you to picture their faces?

    (a) You remember most of them.
    (b) You remember a few of them.
    (c) You seldom remember any of them.

6. In your early school days, how easy was spelling and the writing of essays?

    (a) Both were quite easy.
    (b) One was easy.
    (c) Neither was easy.

7. You spot a parking place but you must reverse into it—and it's going to be a fairly tight squeeze:

    (a) You look for another space.
    (b) You back into it . . . carefully.
    (c) You reverse into it without much thought.

8. You've spent three days in a strange village and someone asks you which way is north:

    (a) You're unlikely to know.
    (b) You're not sure, but given a moment you can work it out.
    (c) You point north.

9. You're in a dentist's waiting room with half a dozen people of the same sex as yourself. How close can you sit to one of them without feeling uncomfortable?

    (a) Less than 6 inches
    (b) 6 inches to 2 feet
    (c) More than 2 feet

10. You are talking to your new neighbor. There's a tap dripping gently in the background. Otherwise the room is quiet:

    (a) You notice the sound immediately and try to ignore it.

    (b) If you notice it, you probably mention it.

    (c) It doesn't bother you at all.

Scoring the Test

Male's score:
Each (a) = 10 points
Each (b) = 5 points
Each (c) = -5 points

Female's score:
Each (a) = 15 points
Each (b) = 5 points
Each (c) = -5 points[5]

Most males will score between 0 and 60. Most females—around 80 percent—will score between 50 and 100. If a male scores above 60, right-brain dominance *may* be indicated. If a female scores below 50, left-brain dominance *may* be indicated.

But for the majority, males tend to favor the left side of the brain, which is factual, lecturing, logical and conquering. While females use both sides of the brain, they tend to favor the right side, which is more feelings- and emotions-based. The right side of the brain is more creative and innovative. It's also where we reach out and touch others in a desire to relate to them in an intimate, loving way.

Do you know which muscles move significantly in a little girl right after birth? Her lip muscles. One of the many great things women often give is a greater awareness and an ability to intimately communicate. God has wired women to be great communicators.

Women are also less aggressive, while men are more aggressive. Even as young boys, we tend to start more fights. On average, males have more violent dreams than females, while women have more romantic dreams than men. Men tend to be more difficult to teach, argumentative and boastful. They have more stuttering problems and issues with learning to read. And they tend to be sicklier. These differences have tremendous implications in the average home.

The Five Key Differences that Build Security

Over the years, we have identified five significant differences between men and women—differences meant to strengthen a relationship but which, if misunderstood, can undermine a healthy marriage.

1. Men Tend to Discover and Express Facts, While Women Tend to Express Intuition and Their Emotions

A study recorded every sound that came from the mouths of a group of little boys and girls aged two to four years old. The researchers discovered that 100 percent of the noises coming out of the little girls' mouths had something to do with conversation, either with herself or someone else. Only 60 percent of the noises coming out of the little boys' mouths had anything to do with conversations; in fact, almost half were just like car noises![6] Those findings can be translated right into a marriage: The wife will ask, "Can we talk tonight, honey?" and the man will make car noises.

Often when a guy gets home from work, he's already used up most of his words—while his wife is just getting started. The woman will want to talk, and the man will ask, "What do you want to discuss?"

The woman responds, "Nothing specific—let's just talk."

Or a man may choose to talk about the facts—as long as there are facts to discuss. As soon as the facts run out, so does the conversation. The woman thought she was just getting warmed up when the conversation peaks because the man ran out of facts to discuss.

Many men find it difficult to discuss things that have to do with relationships or feelings. A woman may ask, "How do you feel about your work?" The man will be tempted to offer the standard response, "I feel fine." The reason? Many men aren't comfortable talking about their feelings and don't know how to respond.

Amy and I (Ted) usually hit the bed around 10 P.M. There are some days when my words run out by noon, especially on Sundays after teaching twice in the morning or on a Saturday after speaking at a conference. On many of those nights, Amy retires to the bedroom with a surplus of 5,000 words remaining. When the lights go out, she starts downloading. The fun part for us now is that she does not expect me to generate a new, fresh 5,000 words. I just get to listen. This understanding has decreased late-night fights for us. All Amy asks is that I reserve a portion of my word count for her every day; she doesn't want me to give away all of my words outside the home.

2. Men Tend to Look for Solutions, While Women Tend to Look for Compassion, Empathy and Understanding

Every so often, my (Gary's) grown daughter visits our house and says, "Dad, can we just talk?" We sit down in the living room and she starts talking. At times, I honestly struggle to follow what she's saying. *Does she need me to give fatherly advice? Does she need me to fix something? Does she need my help?* Finally I ask her, "Kari, are we talking about anything specific?"

"I just wanted to hang with you, Dad," she responds.

When I hear those words, I know that I can just relax and enjoy the time of being with her. Or consider a common activity like shopping. A woman will say, "Do you want to go shopping?" The man will say, "Sure—I'll go with you." Now for the women in my house, it's not just shopping but *s-h-h-o-o-p-p-p-i-i-n-n-g*.

I learned this early on in our marriage. We'd go to the largest mall in the area and I would always want to know what we were looking for. If Norma said we were looking for new shoes, then we'd head into the first store and she'd try a few on.

I'd say, "Those look great. Are they comfortable? Let's get them." And do you know what she would do? She'd put them back on the shelf and head to the next department store, where she'd try on similar shoes. I'd find some that looked great and suggest she buy two pairs. But she'd keep putting them back on the shelf. After an hour or so of shopping, guess what she wanted to do? Stop and enjoy some coffee and some conversation!

Meanwhile, I couldn't even concentrate because we didn't have any shoes. In fact, I was no longer shopping for shoes—I was *hunting* for shoes. I wanted to shoot the shoes, bag them and get out of there.

That's one of the big differences between us. But over the years I've actually trained myself not just to shop but to go *s-h-h-o-o-p-p-p-i-i-n-n-g*. We even trained our boys, and we can make it more than two hours now! I made a decision to learn to like shopping because I know how special it is to my wife. It's something we can do together, and it's one of the ways I can honor her. And there are a lot of conversations that take place in a mall that don't happen anywhere else.

3. Men Tend to Be Objective, While Women Tend to Be Personal

In a lot of ways, men are like the inside of a ship. We are compartmentalized. We go to one room and shut the door. Then we go into another room and shut the door and so on. Women are more like a river. They flow. The past, the present and the future all flow together.

Sometimes a man will come home from work and the wife will ask, "Did you think about me today?" The man will respond, "Well, let me think. I'm sure I did." Generally, men tend to compartmentalize. When they're at work, they're at work; when they're at home, they're at home.

When Amy and I (Ted) are driving down the road, she occasionally glances over at me and asks, "What are you thinking about right now?" This always catches me off guard. She has a hard time believing that men can park their brains in neutral and be thinking about absolutely nothing. I usually find something quick to say: "We need an oil change in 400 miles." (That little sticker in the upper left-hand corner of the windshield was the first thing I saw.) Ladies, let me share with you an important fact: If you are ever wondering whether or not your husband is thinking about the relationship, he's not.

On the other hand, consider an afternoon football game on television. Why is it easy for many women to walk right by? They don't know anyone on the field. They have no personal relationship with the players. How do you get a woman to watch a football game? Introduce them to the players, not as statistics, but as real people. Use *Sports Illustrated* or find interviews with the individual players to find out about their backgrounds, families and children. Then the next time you're watching a game, you can say, "That player who just threw the ball—he's the one with twins. The guy who caught it—he's the one whose mom survived breast cancer." You'd be amazed how much more your wife enjoys a game when you personalize it for her!

4. A Lot of Men Can Separate Who They Are from Their Surroundings, but the Home Is an Extension of Most Women

Amy and I bought our first home in 1998, while I was attending seminary in Dallas. It was one of those $90,000 cookie-cutter homes in a subdivision of 200 homes. We got to choose some upgrades, but most of the features of the home were the basic starter fixtures.

One night shortly after moving in, Amy and I were enjoying an evening at home, watching one of our favorite television programs. Halfway through the program, Amy jumped up and announced, "I can't sit in this living room one more minute!"

"What's wrong?" I asked.

"Doesn't it bother you that the doorknobs in this room are polished brass and the ceiling fan is brushed nickel? What were the builders thinking?" she exclaimed.

My eyes focused on the fan, then the door, then the fan and then the door in rapid fire. I could not process what had her so alarmed. We had just been wrapped up in the suspense of a good crime show when she made this announcement. I had no idea that for the first 30 minutes of the show, Amy could not focus on the plot or the characters because of the mismatched doorknobs and ceiling fan.

Any idea what our first errand was on the following Saturday? You guessed it: We were at Home Depot purchasing brushed-nickel doorknobs. Amy was at peace. Well, she was until she walked into the bedroom that night. You see, the new doorknob was on a door between our bedroom and the living room. And the ceiling fan in our master bedroom was polished brass. On Sunday we were back at Home Depot buying a brushed-nickel ceiling fan for our room.

For many women, the home is an extension of who they are, and the little details can make a big difference when it comes to their comfort level.

Have you ever been headed out the door and heard your wife say, "Oh, I forgot to wash the dishes" or "I didn't make the bed"? It's really hard for a woman to just walk out when things are undone. It's almost as if a part of *her* is undone. I can leave the house without worrying about the dishes, but she can't. When I understand this difference, I am better equipped to love and serve her in a way that makes her feel comfortable and more secure in our relationship and home.

5. Men Tend to Focus on the Basics, While Women Tend to Focus on Details that Make Up the Big Picture

Women go through life experiencing things on both sides of their brains. They experience things logically as well as emotionally. When people's experiences touch their emotions, the experiences are easier to remember. For instance, students who study information using their right brain and feelings tend to remember the information for a longer period of time and in greater detail.

If a son goes off to college, the dad might call and ask, "How are you doing? Do you have enough money? Are your classes okay? Have you met any friends? Good. Have a great time!" Then he hangs up. Now if the mom calls, she'll probably ask, "How are you doing? What's your room like? Tell me about your roommate. Your friends. Your professors. The food." She'll take the conversation to a whole new level.

Getting our children ready to go out the door has always been a struggle. The struggle does not lie in the stuff we need to get out the door but rather in the frustration Amy and I have toward each other as we gather the stuff.

For me, leaving the home with our two-year-old and four-year-old is easy: Get the kids' shoes on and buckle them in their seats.

For Amy, her checklist is just a bit longer. Her list includes hair and teeth brushed; collars down and all buttons buttoned; no obvious stains; diaper bag filled with juice boxes, diapers, wipes, changes of clothes, banana, apple, extra hair clips and toys to entertain the kids.

Here's the rub: Amy and I plan a time to connect for dinner after she has a meeting at the church on a Saturday. That means I am at home with the kids, fully responsible for their preparation to go out for dinner. Being a guy, and at times disassociated from details, I don't have a list. Corynn, Carson and I show up for dinner, and Amy's shock is not hidden. Carson has a grape-juice box stain from lunch on his shirt. Corynn's shorts do not match her shirt. Amy asks, "Where's the backpack?"

"I knew I forgot something," I confess.

Understanding this fifth difference between men and women has created greater security in our marriage. Now I work to honor her checklist and show up with the kids a little better put together. Amy has learned to laugh, knowing that I tried.

The Marriage Manual

We have never met a woman who doesn't have a built-in marriage manual. A husband has a gold mine of natural relational knowledge right in bed with him! Even if she was abused as a child, teased as a teen or put down by relatives, she can still pull out her built-in manual for you if you are safe and caring.

This is one of the very best things about women: They have an innate desire for great relationships. It must have been placed there by God Himself. That means that any man can tap into his wife's built-in marriage manual anytime he wants by asking three questions:

1. *On a scale of 1 to 10, what kind of a marriage do you want?* Usually a woman will say a 10 or something close to it. I've never met a woman who will say, "I want a marriage that's a 2 or 3." No one wants to get married and be miserable.

2. *On a scale of 1 to 10, where is our marriage today?* Now here's what's interesting: In our studies, most women answer the question more accurately than the average man. On average, a man will answer the question two to four points higher than the

average woman. That's why men are often surprised to hear what their wives really think about their marriage. But no matter what answer a woman gives on this question, what's really important is the third question! (But you probably won't make it to the third question unless you continue to be safe for her while she talks.)

3. *What would it take today or in the next few weeks to move our relationship to a 10?* Any couple can use these three questions of the marriage manual to transform their relationship! Now it's important to ask the questions with an attitude of humility and with a desire for personal and relational growth. You need to be ready to hear an honest answer from your spouse. If you respond with, "I can't believe you just said that," then your spouse is going to be tempted to shut down. Be gentle and honor your spouse with a commitment: "I am really serious about our relationship. I may not understand what you mean right now, but I'm committed to understanding you and taking our relationship to a 10."

I have seen couples' marriages revolutionized in a matter of an hour by being able and willing to ask these questions.

Overcoming the Differences

Did you know that the human brain is so fabulous and powerful that the average person only uses 8 percent of the brain's mental capacity? That means that we all have the ability to grow and change in our cognitive abilities and relational skills. If you tend to favor the left or right side of your brain, you can learn to use the other side! Every man and woman has tremendous potential!

So why not begin today? Raise the value of your mate close to 10. Honor your love. Make your spouse feel secure. And keep making the decision to value your mate every day. Even if you don't feel like it initially, rest assured that your feelings will catch up with your attitudes and choices. And before you know it, you'll have a 10 marriage. And that 10 includes your sex life, as we'll discover in the upcoming chapters on foreplay, connection and creativity.

From GarySmalley.com

Q: *I have been reading a book that is opening my eyes to the way men think. To be perfectly honest, I get frustrated when I think about men being turned on by what they see. My husband and I have had some intense discussions about this. I have asked him point blank if he lusts. Our conversations usually lead back to the fact that all men are tempted in this area. First of all, is this true? If so, what can be done to protect my husband from this temptation?*

A: The answer is yes to your first question. Dallas Seminary professor Howard Hendricks has been quoted as saying, "If a man is not tempted to lust, then he's got another problem."

There are many common misunderstandings about temptation. The fact is that temptation is not sin. God is not disappointed and displeased with us when we are tempted. To be strongly tempted does not mean we are as guilty as if we had actually committed sin. The most spiritually mature followers of Christ are tempted.

Temptation is common to all Christ-followers. The Bible encourages us, "But remember this—the wrong desires that come into your life aren't anything new and different. Many others have faced exactly the same problems before you" (1 Cor. 10:13, *TLB*). It is also important to remember that God does not lead us into temptation. James 1:13 says, "When tempted, no one should say, 'God is tempting me.' For God cannot be tempted by evil, nor does he tempt anyone." Temptation itself is not sin, but acting on it is. No temptation is irresistible.

Temptation is one thing, but lusting for a woman other than your mate is imagining in your mind the entire sexual act. I believe that masturbating while dreaming of being with someone other than your spouse is what Christ says is "adultery" (Matt. 5:28). Longing for sexual intimacy with another woman is dreaming of being with her and releasing yourself sexually during the dream. Adultery is breaking the deal you made with your wife and God to not have any other woman in your mind and heart while married.

Understanding the temptations that confront both men and women brings greater security to the marriage. Guarding our hearts from these temptations is one more way to honor your mate. Communicating the steps we take in guarding our hearts is a key to security.

Scripture gives us great encouragement when it says, "You can trust God to keep the temptation from becoming so strong that you can't stand up against it, for he has promised this and will do what he says. He will show you how to escape temptation's power so that you can bear up patiently against it" (1 Cor. 10:13, *TLB*). Jesus was there before us. He was tempted, too. Hebrews 4:15 says, "For we do not have a high priest who is unable to sympathize with our weaknesses, but we have one who has been tempted in every way, just as we are—yet was without sin."

That's why it's so important to guard our hearts. Saying no to temptation is saying yes to something far better. The fact that you and your husband are discussing this issue is a good thing. Avoid a judgmental spirit. If your marriage is healthy, vulnerable and growing in intimacy, you can play a huge role in curbing his temptation to lust.

Notes

1. Anne Moir and David Jessel, *Brain Sex: The Real Difference Between Men and Women* (New York: A Delta Book/Dell Publishing, 1989), p. 9.
2. Ibid., p. 5.
3. Ibid., n.p.; also Louann Brizendine, M.D., *The Female Brain* (New York: Morgan Road Books, 2007), n.p.
4. Moir and Jessel, *Brain Sex: The Real Difference Between Men and Women*, p. 40.
5. Ibid., pp. 50-52.
6. Robert Kohn, "Patterns of Hemispheric Specialization in Preschoolers," *Neuropsychologia*, 12:505, p. 12.

Summary

Intimacy in a relationship begins by establishing honor and security, not by demanding respect.

Discovering true intimacy begins with understanding the unique, God-created differences between men and women.

If you honor your spouse and make him or her feel secure, you will be on the road to true intimacy.

Pillow Talk

On a scale of 1 to 10, what kind of a marriage do you want?

On a scale of 1 to 10, where is our marriage today?

What would it take today or in the next few weeks to move our relationship to a 10?

What key differences have been causing conflict in our marriage?

What steps can we take to celebrate those differences?

CHAPTER 5

The Secret to Great Sex

When Amy and I (Ted) were first married, I never could quite figure out how to get my wife in the mood. We both worked all day and then came home to prepare dinner and complete various chores around the house. I was ready for sex around 9 P.M., but there were many nights when Amy was not.

I used my imagination to come up with a list of reasons why my wife wasn't feeling frisky:

Her boss had overloaded her with extra work.

She was tired from teaching kids all day.

Dinner had upset her stomach.

It was *that* time of the month.

She forgot to have her quiet time.

Notice that I was nowhere on the list. There was no possible way that I could be part of the reason that my wife was not in the mood. After all, getting in the mood was her responsibility, not mine.

I was such a fool!

It wasn't until I watched Gary Smalley's DVD series *Homes of Honor* that I started to figure this out. In the series, Gary describes men as fast to respond to sex while women seemed to need time to warm up. I didn't realize that for women, sex begins in the morning.

Before watching *Homes of Honor*, I struggled with sex for the first seven years of my marriage. I had no idea that the secret to great sex was found in listening and communication. I didn't know that honor leads to security, which leads to intimacy, which results in sex.

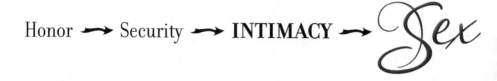

Honor ➤ Security ➤ **INTIMACY** ➤ *Sex*

Now I know that great sex starts in the heart, not between the legs. Since that realization, Amy and I have had far greater sexual intimacy—not because we have learned new positions or techniques, but because we have learned how to connect emotionally through communication.

Whenever we teach communication at conferences, Gary and I always have couples married 20 or more years approach us and say, "We wish we would have learned this stuff when we were first married." So whether you're engaged or getting ready to celebrate your twenty-fifth wedding anniversary, knowing the six levels of communication described here will set you on a course to the best sex of your life. And you'll discover that intercourse is much more than just physical—it's also mental and emotional.

The Six Levels of Communication

Great communication isn't just a matter of *what* you say but *how* you say it. For instance, you can say the word "woman" a lot of different ways. You can say, "Woman," or "WOMAN!" or "Whoooa-man." It's one word, but we add so much to it through our tone, vocal inflection, rate of speech and facial expression.

> *The best communication of your life begins when your desire to understand your mate is greater than your desire to be understood.*

As you study the following, consider your family members, your friends and even your own spouse: With which levels of communication are you most comfortable?

Level 1: Small Talk

Small talk is the level you use with perfect strangers. You may say, "Hey, how are you doing?" And they say, "I'm great!"—often whether or not it's true. Small talk is what we use to communicate with people we don't really know, like grocery-store clerks, waiters and other people we run into while going about our day. In marriage, some couples move into this level when angry with each other or bored. It's the least satisfying level of communication and can kill any remaining love you have left.

Level 2: Facts

This level invites people to exchange facts surrounding their lives. "Do you know what the weather forecast is for the weekend?" "Did you hear the breaking news story on Fox News?" "How was your lunch?" There's either very little or no tension found in these first two levels of communication in most marriages. But conflict can creep in. A couple may start arguing over facts such as, "I told you dinner was at 6 P.M.," and the retort, "No, you said 7 P.M. this morning as clear as ever! I'm sick of you changing the time, I'm starved, and I'm going to Wendy's. Do whatever you want."

Don't ever waste your relationship over misunderstood facts. Any angry discussion instantly weakens the marriage relationship because you're violating the fundamental principle of marriage: *United as one.* (In chapter 11, we'll teach you to resolve conflict before it starts.)

Level 3: Opinions

This third level of communication is where things can get a little dicey. This is where we begin to risk conflict about something we all have— opinions. At this level of communication, you naturally move from stating facts to assessing them. When two people exchange opinions, they immediately recognize the differences and risk disagreement, increased tension and the potential for angry arguments. Here is the real test for honor and security. When you come to the place of highly valuing your mate's opinions as theirs and not yours, you'll begin to see much more deeply within the heart of your mate. Respect for anyone's personal, private opinions leads to some of the deepest connections. Such connections between two people who are married can lead to the absolute best sex! When women feel understood and respected for their opinions, they melt in their husbands' arms. Discovering and respecting each other's opinions will lead to a much deeper relationship.

Level 4: Feelings

If you can manage to exchange opinions in a healthy, mature way, showing respect and even appreciation for the differences between the two of you, communication will often go one level deeper: You'll begin to exchange feelings. You begin to open your emotions to someone else. This is a particularly sensitive level in communication, because if you share your feelings on a matter and are told that you're wrong, you can naturally feel disconnected from your spouse. Depending on the situation and response, you may also feel rejected, abandoned or controlled. Depending on your levels of security and self-worth, you may even feel like a failure. Healthy communication between couples should get to this level and beyond, but often this is where it gets stuck. Whenever feelings aren't exchanged in a healthy way, one or both people in a relationship get hurt, undermining the ability to communicate. That's why it's crucial to never react negatively to your own feelings or someone else's. Just listen in order to better understand.

Level 5: Needs and Desires

When couples feel secure sharing their feelings, they can take their communication further and begin to exchange needs. This is where we begin to discuss our feelings about what we really want and desire from our mate. This level of communication requires a strong sense of honor and security. You must be able to share your opinions, feelings and deepest needs without fear of judgment, criticism or blame if you ever want the deepest levels of love and respect in your relationship. Reaching this level of communication in a marriage results in intimacy. But you can still go one level deeper.

Level 6: Beliefs

Beliefs reflect the core of who you are. Your beliefs track back in your heart for years—even back to childhood. Your beliefs—also known as the messages on your heart—have been a part of you for a long time and reflect who you really are.

Your words and reactions flow straight from your heart. Your heart contains your core beliefs. The way you dress in the morning flows from your beliefs (whether you are secure or insecure with your body), as does the way you eat. Everything about your life rests in this sixth level. Couples with the greatest sexual intimacy have learned this secret. They have made it to this level and have cultivated great communication by listening to each other's hearts.

A desire is something we seek from our spouse, while a belief is the nugget that drives our feelings and desires. When we get to the why (belief), it gives us the heart to do the how (desire).

As you reflect on the six levels of communication, it's crucial to remember that the goal is to reach the sixth level of communication as often as possible. The ultimate goal is to understand each other on all levels—but especially the sixth.

I (Gary) used to think that the goal was to be understood by my mate. I thought good communication in marriage happened through everyday conversation. I thought I was a good communicator when I convinced my wife of something. If I had a great argument or persuasive speech, I thought we were communicating. Boy, was I wrong! Great communication is founded on honoring your spouse and developing security in the relationship. It begins with listening, blossoms into sharing and ends in understanding rather than just being understood.

One of the wisest and most successful men who ever lived was King Solomon. He wrote sections of Scripture that changed me forever. Proverbs 4:23 says, "Above all else [the first thing you do each day for the rest of your life], guard your heart, for everything you do flows from it" (*TNIV*). When I discovered that my deepest beliefs are stored within my heart, I began to manage my beliefs—and as a result, my life has become more enriched than from anything else I have ever done. And as my wife has begun to more deeply understand my new beliefs, we have grown closer and more in love than at any other time in our 43 years of marriage.

The real test of listening and remaining on the best and deepest three levels of communication is when the two of you have a different opinion about some important topic that needs a decision. Great sex begins with taking the time to first listen to your mate and understand as many things about him or her as you can. Listening is honoring. Listening is security, especially when you don't react, but instead become genuinely curious and fascinated by what your mate is saying to you. "Oh, so that's what you mean" or "I always wondered what you believed about that."

Setting the Stage for the Best Communication

Because God, not your spouse, is ultimately your life source, there are times each day when you need to remind yourself of this important fact. One of the worst things you can do is expect your mate to be your god. Your mate will never match up to God. We can't expect our mate to meet all of our needs—that's God job. This allows us to relax with the person we married and build the relationship God intended us to have without the expectation that our mate will fulfill us or become our soul mate. God is our true soul mate. Our mate is our best friend with all of the human weaknesses everyone has. So you can't wait for your love to do the right thing or even respond in the right way. It begins with you. If you're caught in a situation in which your spouse is exploding over something small, pause and take a deep breath; then let your words be few and let them be seasoned with grace and love. As you think about your response, here are a few things to consider as you treasure hunt for the heart issues:

Use and Read Body Language
Communication has more to do with body language than it does with words. We communicate more by the way we say something than the

words that we use. The next time you're talking with your spouse over a potentially hot issue, study his or her body posture. Is he turned away from you? Is she intentionally distracted? How far away from you is he? The other side of the couch? The other side of the room? Even if your spouse isn't saying anything verbally, communication is still going on. Learn to read body language.

Restate Words

Don't restate *your* words—restate your love's words. One of the best ways to deepen communication is to take what your love says and repeat it back by using different words. This will help ensure that what is being said is really what you're hearing. When spoken with gentleness, such restatements create an atmosphere of understanding and healthy communication.

Use Encouraging Signals

Look for opportunities to respond to your spouse positively through your physical response. Sit close. Hold hands if appropriate. Offer a positive nod or verbal affirmation such as "Yeah," "Uh-huh" or "Oh" when appropriate. Obviously, you won't want to respond this way with every sentence, but every so often in a conversation, it can be extremely helpful.

Be Specific

Proverbs 13:17 tells us, "Reliable communication permits progress" (*TLB*). That's why it's so important to be specific. Tell your spouse what's on your heart and in your heart. If you feel uncomfortable with something, let your spouse know. Even if you're discussing a difficult subject like why your spouse doesn't want to have sex, remember to stay focused on the issue. There are lots of reasons why your spouse may say "Not tonight." Some are biological. Some are hormonal. Some are caused by side effects of medication. Some may come from emotional baggage or scarring. I once counseled a man who didn't understand the frigidness of his wife until she dropped the bombshell that she had been sexually abused as a child. That's why communicating our desires is so important.

Maintain Eye Contact

Our eyes have been described as the window to our soul. They reveal more about us than we can ever imagine! That's one reason why maintaining eye contact is so important. In my (Ted's) relationship with Amy, I've discovered that if we're in a deep conversation and I break eye contact for even half a second, I unintentionally undermine everything I've just said. My lack of eye contact communicates that I'm distracted and disconnected, even if I'm not. I have to be intentional about focusing on her and acknowledging what she is saying. Maintaining eye contact creates a more secure atmosphere, particularly when you're communicating your feelings, needs and beliefs. It's in these moments in our marriage that I'm still finding myself saying, "Wow—I never knew that about you before!"

Set the Scene

Great communication requires removing the distractions. That means turning off the television, cell phone and computer. You may be tempted to leave the television on mute and the cell phone on vibrate, but it's best to turn them off completely.

One of the best times of communication for Amy and me is around 9 P.M., after the kids are in bed. We make a pot of Dunkin' Donuts decaffeinated coffee, sit in the downstairs family room on the sectional and spend time connecting. Usually by that time of day, I'm out of words and have little else to say—but that's a good thing, because I'm more apt to be a better listener.

Even if the scene for communication isn't ideal, I can make an effort to improve it. For instance, sometimes right after we turn off the lights for bed, my wife comes up with something she wants to talk about or share. Which is great, except for the fact that within minutes of my head hitting the pillow, I'm snoring. So if Amy begins to talk, I either turn on the light and look at her or do everything I can to stay awake and offer her verbal affirmation. I don't want to miss these moments and the opportunity to live at a Level 6 of communication in my marriage.

As you make your way each day toward the sixth level of communication and find yourselves having much better sex as a result, you may begin to realize that intercourse is more than just physical—it's also mental and emotional.

Mental Intercourse

Early in my (Gary's) marriage, I didn't know anything about cultivating a great sex life. Did my dad ever have a talk with me? Nope. Did my mom? Negative. Sex was a taboo subject around our house. I learned everything I knew about sex from my buddies, and they didn't know much. When I started discovering that sex was a reflection of a good relationship and that intercourse begins with mental intercourse, it transformed my marriage.

A while back, Norma and I took our first trip to Hawaii. I expected the trip to be full of beaches, sun and romance. One day I decided to spend the day doing what my wife loves—touring the island. We had an amazing day together exploring small towns and various shops. We were connecting, sharing and enjoying each other. We were having mental intercourse. As the sun began to set, it was time to head back to the hotel.

When I looked at the gas gauge, I discovered that it was past empty. I didn't want anything to disrupt our perfect day, so I decided to quietly pop the car out of gear and use the clutch to coast down the hills to save as much gas as possible. My observant wife noticed something was different and asked, "What's wrong?" I didn't say a word. I just kept thinking, *Keep going. You can make it.* More than anything, I didn't want to break the flow of the day—the enjoyable mental intercourse—we had enjoyed and the evening we were going to share together physically.

As we reached the top of the hill, I pressed my foot down to pop it out of gear. But (slightly distracted by the thought of our night together) instead of pushing in the clutch, I accidentally slammed on the brake. The car skidded to the middle of the road, and my poor wife slammed up against the dash and windshield.

Norma cried out, "What are you doing?" And I'm thinking, *I'm wrecking our great day and the great sex we were going to have tonight.*

I ended up sharing the problem, explaining that I hit the brake instead of the clutch because I was nervous about spoiling our awesome day. She liked that explanation, and the night turned out great after all.

Great mental intercourse almost always leads to even better sexual intercourse. As you go further in your communication with your spouse, you'll find yourself experiencing mental intercourse. Now, we're not talking about pornography or dirty thoughts. Too often, intercourse is understood only as an act or an event, but it's not. People today are having more sex than ever but enjoying it less, and it's this lack of mental intercourse that can even lead to dysfunction and addiction. Intercourse is not an act—it is a reflection of a great relationship.

Honor ⟶ Security ⟶ Intimacy ⟶ *Sex*

Intercourse doesn't mean orgasm or insertion. Intercourse actually means to get to know someone intimately. That's how we have mental intercourse. Now obviously if you use it outside of this context—or try to drop it into a conversation with your neighbor without explanation—it doesn't make sense. The sex life of a couple is a reflection of their relationship. Sex is like picking fruit off of a tree: The fruit must have the total context of nurture—soil, water and sun in a healthy environment—if it's going to multiply and taste good. Good sexual fruit in your marriage comes as a result of nurturing the relationship.

The soil is listening and understanding your mate as he or she feels very honored or valuable to you. The water is touch. The sunlight is security. When you honor your spouse, provide security and create intimacy, sex brings your mate to life. Remember that security is when your mate feels safe to be his- or herself without fear of being blasted by you or judged or criticized. The whole secret to your mutually satisfying sexual experience is creating the safest place on Earth.

I (Gary) have mentioned this story about Norma and me elsewhere, but it's worth repeating. Six years ago when the truth about creating safety in my own home with Norma became my primary goal, I decided to bite the bullet and settle this issue once and forever. I invited Norma to dinner to say something special to her. As we sat at our table, I reached over and took her hand and asked if she could forgive me for all the times I had tried to change her in some way. I told her how wrong I had been in trying to change her, blame her, criticize her and judge her. Doing these things had been the worst thing possible for our marriage and our love for each other. I told her that from that day forward, I would never again try to change her or even criticize her. I would never blame her for "making" me upset or unhappy. If she needed to change something in her life, that would be between her and God, not me. She whispered that she would forgive me, but I could tell she was wary. Past experience with me had taught her to be cautious. She didn't know what I was up to.

Fast-forward five years. Since that night, I have tried not to change Norma in any way. Instead I have praised her just for being herself. I have thanked her many times for warning me in the past, and I have admitted how much better off I would be if I had listened more intently to her in many situations.

Norma feels safer today than she did during the first 40 years of our marriage. She is more willing to share and no longer takes the blame. She now sees our marriage as a judgment-free zone. I hope to keep it that way.

Emotional Intercourse

A wife was taking her husband to the airport. They were running late and speeding down the freeway. The husband looked at the gas gauge and realized that it was close to empty. He suggested they pull over to get more gas.

"Don't worry about it—we'll make it and I'll get some after I drop you off," she said.

"But this is a pretty dangerous area of town," the husband protested. "I don't want to be thinking about you being in any kind of danger while I'm on the airplane. It would relax me to know you're safe and that you know I appreciate all you do for me. You shouldn't have to get the gas."

She reminded him that they were running late, but the husband insisted, "This is really important to me, because you are important to me."

The wife put her hand on his leg and whispered in his ear, "You know what? This conversation is really turning me on."

The Bible's advice on creating the right atmosphere from Song of Songs:

Food (see 2:5)

Complimenting (see 1:15-16)

Great listening (see 2:14)

Slow undressing (see 4:1-5)

Reassurance (see 4:8)

French/Hebrew kissing (see 4:11)

Men want to know, *What turns a woman on?* If it was simply putting gas in a car, the gauge would never drop below full. But it's more than that—it's emotional connection. This woman felt turned on because her husband's actions reflected their relationship. He was concerned about her. He loved her. He wanted to be with her. And he wanted her to be safe.

Picking the richest fruit off of our marriage tree requires knowing each other emotionally. It's not just part of your sexual health; it's also part of your mental, physical and emotional health. Like mental intercourse, emotional intercourse is not an act or event but getting to know someone intimately. And one of the very best ways to know someone as deeply as possible is to learn how to use emotional word pictures. After all, a picture is worth a thousand words.

Emotional Word Pictures

Word pictures can help you communicate your thoughts and emotions. To compare your spouse to a tent, horse or young goat would probably not be a good idea, unless you lived in Solomon's day. When Solomon likened his lover to the mare among Pharaoh's chariots, he was using an emotional word picture to communicate the fact that she was the most important woman in his life.

If you feel as if your spouse doesn't really understand what you say, especially when the subject has to do with emotions, try using a word picture. Here are a few examples:

- *To express your appreciation for your spouse's love:* "Your love for me is like a huge glass of iced tea on a hot summer day. It is cool and crisp, and its refreshment restores my strength and quenches the thirst of my dry, dusty soul."

- *To tell your spouse you feel overlooked:* "When we were first married, I felt like a beautiful, handcrafted, leather-bound, gold-trimmed book that had been presented to you as a gift from God. At first I was received with great enthusiasm and excitement—cherished, talked about, shared with others and handled with care. As time has gone by, however, I've been put on the bookshelf to collect dust. Once in a while you remember I'm here. If only you would take me off the shelf and open me up. If only you would see how much more I have to offer you."

- *To tell your spouse you feel overworked:* "It's like the Super Bowl is over and the players file into the locker room. Dirty uniforms are thrown on the floor, along with dirty socks and muddy cleats. The players shower and slowly file out, leaving me behind. Not only do I have to clean up the mess, but no one even knows I'm here doing it."

If you could express one thought or feeling to your spouse right now, what would it be? To use an emotional word picture, simply connect an interest of your mate with that thought or feeling. It's easy to begin the journey of using emotional word pictures.

A professional football player once came to me and said that his wife was not responding to him. He was extremely frustrated sexually. He had come home quite a few nights in a row and his wife was not interested. I challenged him to give her an emotional word picture so that she could understand what he was feeling. He thought it was a great idea.

He went home and told his wife that he was struggling with their sex life. "I feel like we're playing the cup game," he explained. "It's like there are three cups on our dresser. When I come home, start romancing you and say I want to be involved with you sexually, you tell me to go over to the dresser and check the cups. If I can find the one with the bean underneath, then we get to have sex. If there's no bean, there's no sex. I haven't found a bean in a really long time. I know there's a bean under one of the cups, but during the day it's like you shuffle them around and I never know where to look. I want to know what it will take to have three beans—one under each cup."

The wife responded that she'd love to tell him how to find the bean. She decided to use a different emotional word picture to respond.

"Let's say, I'm like your favorite fishing rod and reel," she said. "When we were first married, how far could you cast me sexually?"

"As far and as often as I wanted," he answered.

"Exactly! But over the last 15 years of our marriage, you've never taken care of the reel. You never washed the saltwater off or oiled it. Now it's all rusty. You never maintained the pole, fixed the eyelets or changed the line. So now what happens when you cast me? It backlashes or gets tangled, right? It's doesn't cast very far and I don't respond."

Realizing the truth in her words, he asked, "How do I get a new rod, reel and line so that we can have the same thing we had when we were younger?"

The woman offered three pieces of advice. First, the husband needed to remove the rust and oil the reel. That meant when he got home after work, he put his arms around her and told her how much she meant to him. It meant inviting her to sit on the couch so that each could talk about their day.

Second, he needed to replace the line. That meant he needed to take time to play with the kids and help them with their homework. That kind of thing turned her on.

"Kids, get in here! I want to play!" the husband interrupted.

And finally, he needed to put a new finish on the pole and replace some of the eyelets. That meant spending time together away from the kids, enjoying each other and connecting mentally and emotionally. Their sexual relationship would be the pleasurable fruit of their relationship.

Do you know what happened? Not only did their relationship and marriage improve dramatically, but also one night after practice, the husband found two beans under one cup!

So what do you need to do to lure your spouse? Is it time to connect mentally? Emotionally? In the next chapter, we're going to give you the tools you need to engage in mental and emotional intercourse. Great sex begins long before you reach the bedroom, as you'll discover as we explore the five secrets of great communication.

From GarySmalley.com

Q: How do I get my husband to talk about himself? We have been married 29 years. The major problem has always been trying to get him to talk about himself—his dreams, goals, desires and things he would like to do. When I ask him about it, he shuts down and says I should change the subject because he isn't going to talk about it, or he feels that it's nothing to talk about. Then I get frustrated and I stop talking to him by only answering with one-liners. I have tried to work it out with him, but I guess I am still going about it the wrong way. Help!

A: If I'm hearing you right, you do not have a deep level of intimacy with your husband. It's not that you want facts, goals and his plans for the future but rather intimacy and emotional connectedness.

In its most basic sense, intimacy is the experience of being close to your husband and openly sharing anything either about yourself or about something else with the confidence of being secure, loved and valued. This may or may not include words. It doesn't necessarily require work or effort. The mistake many make—knowing they want to experience intimacy and that openness is required—is to focus on trying to be open or to create intimacy. Either focus makes getting to true intimacy harder than necessary.

The easier approach to intimacy is to focus on creating a secure environment for yourself and for your spouse. When both of you feel secure, you are naturally inclined to relax and be open. Then intimacy will simply happen.

Openness is the default setting of our hearts. Openness was the natural state of Adam and Eve in the Garden. When spouses are open with each other, intimacy just happens. It does not require effort or conscious attention.

Take a look at your approach. Maybe you have a pattern that has developed without you even noticing. When are you asking him to open up? On weekends? Right after he gets home from work? On the way to run errands? What is your tone? Are you drilling him? Are you frustrated? Look for ways to assure your husband that his dreams, goals and plans are safe with you. They are free from judgment. This is probably just the beginning of discovering new tools for communicating.

Summary

Intercourse doesn't mean orgasm or insertion.
Intercourse means getting to know someone intimately.

The best communication of your life begins when
your desire to understand your mate is greater than
your desire to be understood.

Small talk and *facts* are the more shallow levels
of communication. There is little risk of escalated
conflict at these two levels.

The level of *opinions* is where most couples have
conflict. Most marriages never leave this level.

The deepest three levels—*feelings*, *desires* and *beliefs*—
are where true communication takes place.

Great listeners read body language, restate words,
use encouraging signals and maintain eye contact.

Pillow Talk

If you could express one feeling, desire or belief to me
right now, what would it be?

What level of communication do you think we spend
the most time on?

What will it take for us to live on the levels of feelings,
desires and beliefs?

How can I best get into your heart?

CHAPTER 6

Going Deeper

It's been said that men who bald in the front are great thinkers, men who bald in the back are great lovers, and men who bald in the front and the back (as I'm doing) only think they are great lovers.

I (Gary) once asked my barber if I was going to lose the little bit of hair I had left. I'll never forget his response: "No—it will just redistribute itself in your ears, nose and back as you get older."

No matter what your age and where your hair is or isn't growing, your sex life is a barometer of your relationship with your spouse. It's a reflection of what's going on in your life. It's like the 85-year-old couple that has been married for more than 50 years. When the wife discovered that their sex life was a barometer of their relationship, she knew she had to address the issue with her husband right away. She asked, "George, whatever happened to our sex relations?"

"I think they're fine," he answered. "Didn't we get a Christmas card from them last year?"

In this chapter, we're going to go even deeper into how to experience the best sex of your life. As we discovered in the last chapter, the secret to great sex is communication. Now that you know the six levels of communication, we want to equip you with the five secrets to great communication.

The Five Secrets to Great Communication

1. Listen Slowly

Great communication begins with listening to your spouse. That means spending more time listening than speaking. Consider James 1:19: "My dear brothers, take note of this: Everyone should be quick to listen, slow to speak and slow to become angry." Now *that's* a piece of wisdom every marriage and relationship can benefit from! Notice that the Bible doesn't instruct you to listen quickly, but to be quick to listen until you understand the other person. There's a natural progression in this verse:

1. Slow down your listening until you understand.
2. Be slow to speak.
3. Be slow to anger.

But so often in our relationships, the order of those gets flipped—instead of slowing ourselves, we run headfirst into speaking with anger. Many easily resolvable conflicts escalate because our buttons get pushed and we become angry, and only after we have spewed out of our intemperate hearts are we ready to really listen.

The Bible wisely instructs us to begin by resisting the urge to purge our words. Instead, we're challenged to put our own lips into timeout and respond rather than react. Proverbs 29:20 says, "There is more hope for a fool than for someone who speaks without thinking" (*NLT*). Taking time to listen will improve your communication, your relationship and your marriage.

2. Focus on Feelings, Not Issues

This is a crucial marriage principle to remember: *The issue is rarely ever the issue.*

Sex, in-laws, parenting, kids, friends, work, bosses—a variety of things are blamed for marital strife. However, they are not the *source* of your conflict. They are issues. And issues point to what is happening on the inside.

We've heard couples say that money tore them apart, but money has never caused a single divorce. Some have argued that bankruptcy caused the divorce, but, again, bankruptcy did not cause it. The real cause of the divorce was the fact that the couple only reached the third level of communication. They exchanged opinions but never got down to talking about feelings, needs and beliefs—they never truly understood each other.

When was the last time you had a heart exam? Not a medical heart exam, but a spiritual one? As we mentioned earlier, the Bible instructs, "Above all else, guard your heart, for it is the wellspring of life" (Prov. 4:23). That means we are to stand watch over our hearts. Take a good, close look. It's easy to point to circumstances rather than our own expectations as a source of disappointment and even hurt. Sadly, some people believe that if they just pack up and go to another marriage, things will be better. Until we realize that our heart guides our reactions to our mate, we will not understand the true source of our issues.

In the third year of planting our church, we almost had a fistfight break out in the parking lot of our church in Branson, Missouri. It was between a visitor and a regular attendee. Later in the day, the visitor emailed me (Ted) and said he planned on "whipping the driver silly." He wrote, "I don't blame this guy [the regular attendee who was driving slowly]. I blame you because I believe people reflect the leadership they are under."

The visitor was talking about me! So I did what any sane pastor would do: I invited him to breakfast. (Don't worry—I had secretly planted some "bodyguard" friends around the restaurant. I wanted to be protected.) For the last several weeks, I've been meeting with this "crazed" driver. As I have gotten to know him better, I have learned about his heart, and I've discovered that I'm not really this guy's main issue. In fact, the driver that frustrated him on the way to church is not this guy's main issue. Neither our church nor our leadership team is this guy's main issue. During our breakfasts together, I discovered that this young man's fiancée had broken up with him the previous week. He didn't want to hurt any of us—he wanted to hurt his ex-fiancée.

All of us experience pain and loss in our lives. Some scars run deeper than others. Teachers, coaches, bosses, neighbors, strangers and even family members may say or do inappropriate or cruel things. Some of their words or actions may be abusive or destructive. But remember that even though you may have been victimized, you can make the choice to no longer be a victim.

To have someone who understands our deepest feelings about past circumstances is so important in our longing to be loved. We all have the deep need to be loved. When our love "bucket" is not being filled or if it never was, we tend to react to people in negative ways without knowing the source of our reaction.

In the same way, someone's negative reaction to you is more than likely related to the level of love that person is experiencing in life. Maybe—just maybe—when your mate is reacting to you, you should listen carefully to hear how much love he or she has been receiving from you lately.

I make it a habit to always listen to how much love others are receiving instead of taking their words at face value—or worse, taking them as personal attacks on me. As soon as I start watching facial expressions and listening to the tone and feelings behind the words, I become a much better listener. How many times have you listened to someone attacking you and reacted in anger because their words made it sound as if something is wrong with you? People continually tell you what they believe, need or desire by the way they talk. Words say more about the person saying them than about the person listening.

I began to listen better to my mate and others when I discovered that I don't need to take personally everything that comes out of someone else's mouth. When I feel attacked, I've discovered a way to fight back (and it's probably not what you think!). I call it treasure hunting. Treasure hunting is finding out what's really going on in the other person's heart.

For the first seven years of my marriage to Amy, I would often say things in reaction to my wife that were unkind and sometimes even cruel. I would shut down my heart and mind, refusing to hear what she was saying. But slowly over time, she would pry her way into my heart. She wanted to know what was really going on. And so often, the disagreement we were having or the anger I was expressing didn't really have to do with the issue at hand.

Everything about you—what people see on the outside—is just a reflection of what is going on in your heart. Proverbs 27:19 says, "As water reflects a face, so a man's heart reflects the man." And Proverbs 23:7 says, "For as he thinks in his heart, so is he" (*AMP*). I'm slowly discovering that when people fall into attack mode, I need to figure out what's really going on inside. What's the real issue? Where is the anger coming from?

When was the last time you were in a restaurant and the wait staff or cashier was on edge? Did you take it personally? How did it affect your attitude toward the person? Treasure hunting means not taking offense but pressing deeper into the heart of the person. This may mean simply stopping the person and asking, "How's your day going?" or "What's the matter?" or offering an encouraging comment like, "It sure is busy today, but you're holding it together really well." You will be amazed at what comes out of a person's heart after just a few words or moments of kindness.

Treasure hunting means trying to understand where people are coming from and giving them grace for their less-than-pleasant moments—because we all have them.

Treasure hunting works in all different circumstances and intersections of life. For example, if I see a man express aggression or road rage while I'm driving, I think he may have had a fight with his spouse before getting behind the wheel this morning. Or maybe the driver's dad doesn't love him very much. Or maybe the driver's mom said he would never amount to much. Or maybe he suffers from sleep apnea and happens to be grouchy from lack of sleep. Treasure hunting means trying to understand where people are coming from and giving them grace for their less-than-pleasant moments—because we all have them.

That's why it's so important to treasure hunt in your relationships—especially with your spouse. I've seen this play out time and time again in my own marriage.

For instance, for Amy, a birthday party is a really big deal. So when our child had her first birthday, my wife went shopping. And she spent more than $300 on the party. I freaked out! I thought $300 was way too much for a birthday party—especially for a one-year-old. If we would have stayed at level three in our communication and only exchanged our opinions, the issue would have escalated into a full-blown fight. But instead we took time to communicate and talk about our feelings, needs and beliefs.

The Six Levels of Communication in Everyday Conversation

SMALL TALK	Amy: "How was your day?" Ted: "What did you do today?"
FACTS	Amy: "I went shopping today and spent $300 on Corynn's birthday party."
OPINIONS	Ted: "$300 is too much!" Amy: "No, it's not."

FEELINGS	Ted: "I'm worried about paying the bills this month." Amy: "I am uncomfortable with having people over for a party and it not looking good."
DESIRES	Amy: "I want Corynn to feel special." Ted: "So do I."
BELIEFS	Amy: "My mom always made birthday parties extra special and big." Ted: "My parents showed love in other ways. Birthdays were not huge."

Birthdays were not larger-than-life galas or royal balls in my household when I was growing up. We went out to dinner and received a gift. But in Amy's home, birthday parties were planned months in advance. She believed birthdays were some of the most important days of the year.

Amy and I have learned so much about each other after the big blowup over Corynn's first birthday party. I learned how special certain events were to her. I learned how much she holds on to memories and wants to create special memories for our children. She loves parties and coordinates them extremely well. All of what I learned came from treasure hunting my wife's beliefs.

Amy learned a lot about me and my family history as well. My dad grew up with parents who worked hard but did not make a lot of money. They struggled most of the time to make ends meet. Birthdays were not thrown out all together, but they were very simple. When my dad started having children (my brother and I), birthdays were celebrated but were not that big of a deal. So my own dad didn't shower us with larger-than-life birthday parties. My parents showed love in other ways. Birthdays were no big deal. Four generations later, I was passing those beliefs on to my daughter.

On the day Amy and I discovered this about my family, the way we talked about money changed forever. We hadn't known that our disagreements went so deep. This simple discovery changed everything. It also helped Amy and me understand why we had so many struggles at Christmas time. She wanted two trees: One for the living room and one for the family room. I wanted the three-foot tree that would make Charlie Brown proud. (In chapter 11, we are going to give you some of the specific tools that you need to resolve conflict no matter what its size or shape.)

What discoveries are awaiting you in your marriage? What have you been fighting about or disagreeing about for years? Is it possible that on a particular subject, you've never moved beyond Level 3 of communication?

> *What discoveries are awaiting you in your marriage?*

Remember that Level 6 of communication—beliefs—is always where you'll find the best sex of your life. It's a matter of moving past the issue to the heart of the issue. First Peter 3:7 instructs, "Treat [your wife] with understanding as you live together" (*NLT*). A modern translation might read, "Find out what makes your love really tick."

One of the best places in the Bible where this principle is illustrated is tucked into 1 Corinthians 8. Among the Corinthians, the practice of sacrificing meat to idols was a really big issue and everyone had different opinions about it. Paul writes, "Now about food sacrificed to idols: We know that we all possess knowledge. Knowledge puffs up, but love builds up" (1 Cor. 8:1). In other words, we all have opinions and we can get feisty about them. But as followers of Jesus, love trumps our opinions. The first three levels of communication—small talk, facts and opinions—all fit into the category of knowledge. But Paul invites us into the area of love that encompasses the last three levels of communication. When we exchange our feelings, desires and beliefs, we are given a tremendous opportunity to put love into action.

Paul demonstrates this in 1 Corinthians 8. He ends up going into an in-depth discussion on why it's okay to eat the meat sacrificed to idols. But he concludes by saying that he will stop eating the meat if it's an issue to the Corinthians; he'll simply let it go (see v. 13). Why? Because he knows that love is the most important thing. In our marriages, we also need to move from issues into the heart of the issues. Everyone possesses knowledge about certain subjects; the point is that you don't let it puff you up. Instead, choose to move deeper into intimacy and love.

3. Know When Not to Speak

If you can't get past exchanging opinions and move to the next level, resist the urge to restate your case. Instead of adding more coals to the fire, add the cool balms of listening and compassion. Proverbs 26:20 says, "Fire goes out for lack of fuel" (*NLT*). The same principle applies to the negativity in our relationships. When we cut off the fuel supply— rash responses, repetitiveness or any sort of edge in our tone—calmness quickly returns.

The main reason we keep emphasizing the importance of remaining in harmony is that sex stinks or is almost nonexistent when a couple is fighting, arguing or, worse, trying to win an argument. Winning an argument is usually the end of sex. Is it worth disconnecting? That's why learning the simple tools of communication is so important for staying in harmony with each other. The deeper the communication and harmony, the more mutually satisfying the sex.

You can practice this key to great communication no matter the size of the issue. Proverbs 13:3 still applies: "He who guards his lips guards his life, but he who speaks rashly will come to ruin." Amy and I (Ted) have issues over toothpaste. It may sound silly, but we have actually had in-depth discussions and exchanged some strong opinions about how toothpaste should be put on a toothbrush and even how much should be used! I like it when the toothpaste is foaming on both sides of my mouth until I can't contain it. I feel cleaner and, besides, it helps clean the lower portion of my face. Amy, the more cultured of us, brushes in a rhythmic pattern and uses smaller amounts of toothpaste. She has tried to explain to me that a pea-drop amount of toothpaste does the job as well as a heaping mound. I disagree—but then again, you'd probably enjoy watching Amy brush her teeth more than watching me.

The Bible says, "A fool shows his annoyance at once" (Prov. 12:16). A fool doesn't take time to think but just blurts words out. Like toothpaste in a tube, words are squeezed out and then can't be stuffed back in. Use the smaller issues—like toothpaste—to practice holding your tongue. That may mean putting yourself in timeout. Such discipline can go a long way toward honoring your spouse. Then when the bigger issues come along, you'll have the wisdom and knowledge of when not to speak.

4. Use Fewer Words

When it's appropriate to speak about an issue, always use the fewest words possible. Remember that less is more. Proverbs 10:19 says, "Don't talk too much, for it fosters sin. Be sensible and turn off the flow!" (*NLT*). Obviously, the Bible is not discouraging healthy, edifying conversation, but I believe it is challenging us to become wordsmiths in our speech. That means choosing our words carefully, which will naturally cause us to use fewer of them.

Do you remember when teachers in English class used to grade your papers? They would circle things in red and remind you not to start every sentence in a paragraph with the same word. Yet so often when we speak, we have a tendency to begin every sentence with the same word, and it's either "I" or "you." We either take things personally or communicate with accusatory language. That's why it's important to use different words. Be creative. Think about different phrases or expressions when you're not facing a conflict. That means if the same issue keeps popping up—like money—use different words and more uplifting words to address a given topic. At the same time, remember to keep your words few. The Bible says, "He who holds his tongue is wise" (Prov. 10:19). Sometimes saying nothing and just listening is the best reply of all!

Norma and I (Gary) are so opposite in the way we communicate. I talk to think, while she thinks and then talks. I don't have the switch that tells the average person, *Maybe I shouldn't say this.* It has been hard for me to keep quiet, but over the years, I've seen how powerful it is to simply listen.

We were recently driving through the mountains of Colorado, arguing about a money issue. The conversation started to heat up, and I didn't like the belittling tone of her voice. I was starting to get mean when James 1:19 flashed into my mind. I was reminded, *Smalley, shut your mouth!* I tried something that amazed me. I just started listening and asking questions. "How much would you pay for a housecleaning person?" I asked.

"Just drop it," she responded.

"No, I'm truly interested in finding out how much the average cleaning person charges per week."

"Oh, about $40 to $60 per visit," she responded. "It was cheaper when I used to use the person with special needs where we lived before, remember?"

"Yes, I remember her," I responded. "I liked her."

"But today, people charge more," she continued.

"Do you have someone in mind?" I asked.

"Yes, but you aren't interested."

"Who is it?"

"Daisy," she said hesitantly.

"Daisy?" I reflected excitedly. "I like her. Why don't you call her when we get back?"

"Just so you know, working full time now has made it more difficult for me to keep the house up," she confessed. "Just having her once a week would really help me keep my mind on work."

"So I'm hearing you say that when the house is dirty or messed up, you have a hard time concentrating at work?" I said, gently repeating what she had said back to her.

"Yes," she agreed.

"That's really interesting, because it could be a total mess and it wouldn't cross my mind during the day," I explained.

"We are really different, aren't we?" Norma observed.

"Yes, but that's how we complement each other," I responded.

The next thing I knew, the atmosphere in the car had changed, and we thoroughly enjoyed the drive and each other. We continued to talk and share and enjoy the harmony of togetherness—all because I took time to really listen.

5. Choose the Right Words

When you use the right words—loving words—you change the atmosphere of your relationship. Proverbs says, "Pleasant words are a honeycomb, sweet to the soul and healing to the bones" (Prov. 16:24). Our words should be used to build each other up. But too often they're used to belittle or demean the other person. Our words flavor our relationships. Do you want your relationship to be sweet? Desirable? Pleasant? Then choose the right words.

The Bible provides some great communication advice when it says, "A gentle answer turns away wrath, but a harsh word stirs up anger" (Prov. 15:1). Some couples can't get beyond Level 3 in their communication simply because one or both people don't feel secure. When our speech is seasoned with gentleness and kindness, the other person naturally feels honored and secure, which invites them to take the conversation deeper.

One of the ways I (Ted) honor Amy is by calling her by the nickname I gave her: "China Plate." I call her that because I want to verbally remind her that I'm not going to treat her like everyday ware—I want her to know she's special to me. After all, we take great care of our china.

We even invested big money in a special piece of furniture to house it. Sometimes I'll text-message or email her and tell my little China Plate that I love her. Choosing the right words in a relationship naturally leads to honor, security and intimacy . . . which, of course, leads to great sex.

In the next chapter, we're going into the bedroom as we teach you how to engage in unforgettable foreplay with your spouse. This is a chapter you won't want to miss!

From GarySmalley.com

Q: *While dating, he was open, sharing his feelings and relaxed with me all the time. He loved being with me. Now, four years into our marriage, there is zero intimacy. He is dead toward me. He never opens up—doesn't say but four or five sentences a day. I am drowning! I want the relationship we once had. I want the intimacy back in our marriage. What do I do?*

A: When married couples are together in a state of openness, intimacy naturally occurs. In its most basic sense, intimacy is the experience of being close to your spouse and openly sharing anything either about yourself or about something else with the confidence of being secure, loved and valued. This may or may not include words. It doesn't necessarily require work or effort. The mistake many make—knowing they want to experience intimacy and that openness is required—is to focus on trying to be open or to create intimacy. Either focus makes getting to true intimacy harder than necessary. The easier approach to intimacy is to focus on creating a secure environment for yourself and for your spouse. When both of you feel secure, you will be naturally inclined to relax and be open. Then intimacy will simply happen.

Here's what I mean by creating a secure environment: When you have a state-of-the-art security system built into a marriage, especially emotionally, opening up is made significantly easier. When you and your spouse know that both of you are committed to creating a secure marriage, you avoid things that would cause hurt in either of you, and you begin building a foundation for a great relationship. Ideally, your home should feel like the most secure place on Earth.

In your quest to have the best of the best in your marriage, I want to encourage you to make creating security a top priority. Start this process by answering some basic questions, using a scale of 1 to 10 (with 10 being the safest): How secure do you feel today to open up and share anything with your mate without the uneasiness of being criticized or judged? How have you made it insecure for your spouse? How have you built security in your marital environment? What do you do in response to your mate when you're feeling insecure?

Would it be safe to say that your husband felt safe and secure with you while dating? Did he feel judged, looked down on or condemned by the words that he chose or the actions that he took? The intimacy you experienced early on was a result of security.

Focus on creating security with your spouse rather than intimacy.

Summary

Spend more time listening than speaking. Slow down
your listening until you understand.

Sex, in-laws, parenting, kids, friends, work, bosses—
a variety of things are blamed for marital strife.
However, they are not the source of conflict.

Know when not to speak. Sometimes silence is healthy.

When you must speak, learn to use the right words.
Loving words can change the atmosphere of
your relationship.

Pillow Talk

Do you feel listened to when you talk with me?

How can I listen better when you are speaking?

When I am describing you to others, what words
would *honor* you?

When I am describing you to others, what words
would *dishonor* you?

CHAPTER 7

Unforgettable Foreplay

Dan didn't spend a lot of time reading books or talking to his fiancée about their honeymoon. He figured he had seen enough movies and talked to enough high-school buddies to know plenty about sex. After all, how hard could it be to have sex when everyone was doing it? He wasn't like a lot of guys these days—he was still a virgin.

I (Ted) met Dan two years before he married Carolyn, and I had the privilege of leading them through their premarital counseling. One of my favorite parts of premarital counseling is taking the guy golfing or fishing a couple of weeks prior to the wedding. During this excursion, we get into the nitty-gritty of marital sex. We discuss everything from premature ejaculation to the pain a woman can experience during her first time (topics rarely addressed in movies or talked about by buddies in the locker room).

"Dan, the chances are pretty good that you won't even make it five minutes before you orgasm," I said.

"What are you talking about?" he exclaimed, caught off guard and grateful that we were the only ones on the golf course that day.

"Well, most guys have not established endurance for sex," I explained. "We heat up fast and we can finish fast. You need to take some steps in preparing yourself and your wife for that first night together."

"What do I do?" Dan asked. I could tell from his expression that Dan wished he had read some books and not just listened to his friends.

"Don't stress," I encouraged him. "I have a secret that a guy shared with me that helped me out big time on our wedding night: Condoms are your best friend on the honeymoon."

"But we are using the pill," Dan protested.

"The purpose of the condoms is not birth control but to give you more endurance. If you can last through her putting it on you (even great men have failed at this), it will allow you to last three to five times longer."

"You've got to be kidding me!" Dan shouted. "I'm not going to the store to buy condoms—that's embarrassing."

"Do you love her?" I asked.

"Of course," Dan responded.

"Then do what's most loving."

Needless to say, Dan's endurance increased dramatically on his honeymoon—bringing pleasure to his new wife and himself. Sometimes I wonder why no one had shared this with Dan before that day on the golf course. This is the kind of thing guys are embarrassed to talk about, but not being able to pleasure the woman of our dreams by bringing her to orgasm is far more embarrassing because it threatens our manhood. (In "Answers to the Biggies" at the end of this book, we'll share ways men and women can prepare for the honeymoon.)

In this chapter, we're going to explore foreplay and what it takes to set the stage for the best sex of your life. You're going to learn about the chemistry of great sex, a blueprint for great sex laid out in Song of Songs 4 and how to deal with some of the common insecurities that can follow men and women into the bedroom.

The Chemistry of Sex

In *The Female Brain* by Dr. Louann Brizendine, a UCLA neuropsychiatrist, she notes that during a male orgasm, the chemical oxytocin is released into the brain. Now here's what's interesting: In women, the same chemical, oxytocin, is released in the brain during a meaningful conversation. That means it can be as exciting and pleasurable for your wife to connect with you emotionally as it is for her to connect with you sexually.[1]

It can be as exciting and pleasurable for your wife to connect with you emotionally as it is for her to connect with you sexually.

The chemistry of great foreplay begins long before you reach the bedroom. It all goes back to that equation:

Honor ➔ Security ➔ Intimacy ➔ *Sex*

Women naturally want to be connected to men. They're designed for it. For women, foreplay starts early in the morning. That means that it's worthwhile for men to get up early to simply be with their wives. Take time to communicate to her that you want to be with her by taking a shower, shaving and brushing your teeth. Then look for opportunities to serve her. Vacuuming can be sexy. For some women, nothing says "I want you" like a few laps around the living room with the Hoover. When you express your love for her during your cleaning time, she hears you telling her that because you value her, you're helping with housework, the kids or whatever she needs to do around the house. It's the sense of honor and love she is feeling from you that furthers her connection with you. The more connected she feels with you, the more she'll desire your touch. Let her chemistry work for you.

Throughout the day, look for opportunities to exchange NSTs (non-sexual touches). Gently grab her hand. Hug her. Listen to her. Ask her about her day. Look her in the eyes and tell her how much you appreciate her. As you honor her and make her feel secure, you'll find that she warms up slowly but steadily until she's ready to go!

But never forget that most women have a built-in radar system that can detect if you are talking with her, helping with housework or touching her just to warm her up for sex. We're talking genuine love and care for the woman God has given you to honor and nurture until death do you part. A woman can tell the difference between when her mate is "smelling for the bedroom" and when you are truly loving her because she is your best friend and lover. If a man lacks the ability to love in a genuine way, that's when God comes in. He is the giver of lasting, amazing love, and He can provide a deep well of genuine devotion to any man who seeks Him.

Song of Songs 4

Lover

¹How beautiful you are, my darling!
  Oh, how beautiful!
  Your eyes behind your veil are doves.
  Your hair is like a flock of goats
  descending from Mount Gilead.
²Your teeth are like a flock of sheep just shorn,
  coming up from the washing.
  Each has its twin;
  not one of them is alone.
³Your lips are like a scarlet ribbon;
  your mouth is lovely.
  Your temples behind your veil
  are like the halves of a pomegranate.
⁴Your neck is like the tower of David,
  built with elegance;
  on it hang a thousand shields,
  all of them shields of warriors.
⁵Your two breasts are like two fawns,
  like twin fawns of a gazelle
  that browse among the lilies.
⁶Until the day breaks
  and the shadows flee,
  I will go to the mountain of myrrh
  and to the hill of incense.
⁷All beautiful you are, my darling;
  there is no flaw in you.
⁸Come with me from Lebanon, my bride,
  come with me from Lebanon.
  Descend from the crest of Amana,
  from the top of Senir, the summit of Hermon,
  from the lions' dens
  and the mountain haunts of the leopards.

⁹You have stolen my heart, my sister, my bride;
   you have stolen my heart
   with one glance of your eyes,
   with one jewel of your necklace.
¹⁰How delightful is your love, my sister, my bride!
   How much more pleasing is your love than wine,
   and the fragrance of your perfume than any spice!
¹¹Your lips drop sweetness as the honeycomb, my bride;
   milk and honey are under your tongue.
   The fragrance of your garments is like that of Lebanon.
¹²You are a garden locked up, my sister, my bride;
   you are a spring enclosed, a sealed fountain.
¹³Your plants are an orchard of pomegranates
   with choice fruits,
   with henna and nard,
¹⁴nard and saffron,
   calamus and cinnamon,
   with every kind of incense tree,
   with myrrh and aloes
   and all the finest spices.
¹⁵You are a garden fountain,
   a well of flowing water
   streaming down from Lebanon.

Beloved
¹⁶Awake, north wind,
   and come, south wind!
   Blow on my garden,
   that its fragrance may spread abroad.
   Let my lover come into his garden
   and taste its choice fruits.

A Blueprint for Great Sex from Song of Songs

Prepare the Room

After 11 years of marriage, Amy and I have introduced something new into our bedroom: music. I have a "lovemaking playlist" on my iPod and a docking station on the nightstand. (For our Baby Boomer and Builder readers, a docking station is not some weird sex toy. It is a set of speakers much like a radio.) The iPod is loaded with songs from every genre of music and every decade since the '70s. From worship music to a little country, it's all on there. It makes for a wonderfully relaxing time.

Prepare the room. Solomon did it. So do I. Here are some practical ways to prepare the bedroom for lovemaking:

1. *Clean the room.* Obviously, a clean room makes for fewer distractions.

2. *Get rid of the baby monitors and anything else that says "baby!"* Remember that you do not want distractions.

3. *Put a dimmer on the light switch.* You can buy a dimmer for less than $10 at your local home-improvement store.

4. *Set the thermostat.* My wife can tell the difference between 70 and 71 degrees. I have lost track of the number of times in our marriage when she has requested that I adjust the temperature from 70 to 71. She does not want to get started with goose bumps.

5. *Add an extra blanket.* Depending on the season, an extra blanket will get you warm fast. It's amazing how you can start out covered up to your neck and then 10 minutes later you are throwing all the blankets off of the bed. Sex is great!

6. *Install a fireplace.* Just kidding! We're trying to keep this list practical. But if you can, do it.

7. *Place candles around the room.* If you're insecure about your body, use votives. A votive in the far corner may cause some squinting, but it allows the imagination to run wild.

8. *Have lotions handy.* A good rubdown is wonderful foreplay.

9. *Plug-in air fresheners.* This brings a sweet aroma to the room.

10. *Have the condom package open on the nightstand.* Nothing is more frustrating than being 20 or 30 minutes into lovemaking and having to struggle to open a little package.

11. *Have towels or robes ready for after.* Prep for clean-up is important. As our friend Dr. Kevin Leman says, "You have not had great sex if you don't need a shower afterward."

Now, you are not going to have sex that lasts for hours all the time (we will talk about quickies in chapter 9), but this list is for those times when you want to make lovemaking extra special.

Affirm Each Other Verbally

Great foreplay begins long before you actually touch and continues once you do. It begins with the words you speak to one another.

In his ancient book, Solomon draws a beautiful picture of what verbally unwrapping one another means. He knows that for every innocent couple, undressing before the one you love is both a gift and a treat. In chapter 4 of Song of Songs, we read about the king's steamy wedding night. The Shulammite woman, his new bride, is going to undress in front of him with the lights on, but he's not going to touch her right away. Instead, he begins talking to her gently, lovingly, "How beautiful you are, my darling! Oh, how beautiful! Your eyes behind your veil are doves. Your hair is like a flock of goats descending from Mt. Gilead" (4:1). That may sound like a strange compliment, but imagine a mountain with an entire herd of goats climbing down, filling every crack and crevice. They're streaming down the face of the mountain—an impressive sight. Consider the wealth they represented. Solomon describes his wife's hair as beautiful and rich. In ancient Hebrew culture, women wore their hair up. So for Solomon to comment on it meant that she was beginning to expose herself to him—taking the pins out her hair. Her long, soft locks fell below her shoulders.

She smiles at him as she's coming alive to him. "Your teeth are like a flock of sheep just shorn, coming up from the washing. Each has its twin; not one of them is alone," Solomon says (4:2). He's basically saying that her smile is breathtaking, showing white, straight, attractive teeth. Then he progresses in his verbal affirmation of her: "Your lips are like a scarlet ribbon; your mouth is lovely. Your temples behind your veil are like the halves of a pomegranate. Your neck is like the tower of David" (4:3).

Not only does she have rosy cheeks, she also carries herself with respect, dignity and joy. By this remark, Solomon doesn't just comment on what he sees but also on what can't be seen with the physical eyes. Solomon affirms her by reminding her not just of her natural beauty but also of her inner beauty: She walks with self-respect and esteem. Nobility radiates from the innermost parts of her being.

What We Want to Hear in the Bedroom

Women Want to Hear	Men Want to Hear
"There is no flaw in you."	"I'm in the mood."
"I love what you are doing to your hair these days."	"Let's mix it up a little tonight."
"I'm more attracted to you today than when we first married."	"Oh yeah, right there."
"You take my breath away."	"That was great."
"I am one blessed guy."	"I got there."

When you're unwrapping one another, it's important to know what your spouse really wants. Solomon taps into this on his wedding night as his wife is undressing. He says to his bride, "Your two breasts are like two fawns, like twin fawns of a gazelle that browse among the lilies" (4:5). As he sees her breasts, he affirms her body. But he does something else—he lets her know the way he is going to approach her.

Where we (the Cunningham's) live, we have about 10 deer that roam our neighborhood freely. We've become so accustomed to seeing them that we've actually named them all. Now when I want to give my daughter a good look at the deer, I have to be careful in my approach. We don't run up to the deer or make loud, rough sounds. Instead, we approach them gently, calmly.

That is the way many women want to be approached. On Solomon's wedding night, he's watching his bride undress and reveal her naked body to him. But he's not going to let out every sexual fantasy that he has ever had on her. Her breasts are like fawns and Solomon is going to approach them tenderly. He's going to be tender and gentle.

The top thing a woman wants from a man is *gentleness*.

The top thing a man wants from a woman is *responsiveness*.

Just as a woman craves gentleness, a man desires that the woman respond to him. That means that when a woman reaches orgasm, the guy wants to know about it. A portion of his pleasure comes from knowing he's pleased his wife.

Pay Attention to Facial Expressions

Your facial expressions during foreplay may be more important than you realize! In her research on the female brain, Dr. Brizendine found that one of the first things the brain compels a girl to do is to study faces. In fact, over the first three months of life, a baby girl's skills in eye contact and mutual facial gazing increase by over 400 percent, whereas facial gazing skills in a boy during this time do not increase at all.[1]

As babies grow older, little girls interpret an emotionless face turned toward them as a signal that they are not doing something right. Isn't that interesting? I (Ted) have noticed that if I'm not careful, I can make my daughter cry unintentionally just with a facial expression. Yet if I make the same face to my son, he'll totally ignore it.

Now here's the clincher: Girls will pursue a person's facial response. In other words, girls tend to grow up thinking that if they do everything just right, they'll get the reaction they expect. That can lead to unhealthy beliefs like "If I do things just right, then he will love me." Can you imagine the negative impact that an unresponsive parent (or an abusive parent or a depressed parent) has on a little girl's developing sense of self?

Think about your facial expressions throughout the day. How do you respond to your spouse? When you begin foreplay, do you look at her? Do you smile? What is your face communicating? Let me give you an actual example of how facial expressions affect foreplay and communication.

One raised eyebrow, a careless roll of the eyes and a half smirk were not part of Janel's definition of sexual intimacy. Mike's slouched posture, crossed arms and huffing were a regular part of our counseling sessions, so I wasn't surprised when his face and body language betrayed him as she explained her desire for romance. Mike was a classic passive-aggressive: He said the right words but never in the right way. He would say the words Janel was looking for but usually with a sarcastic tone. Janel grew tired of Mike's carelessness and got to the point that she didn't even want him saying the words "I love you" anymore.

"Even when he says 'I love you,' I don't believe him," she said. "Contempt and sarcasm are written all over his face."

"Mike, do you know what sarcasm communicates?" I asked.

"I'm just goofing around," Mike responded, his eyes darting to the floor.

"I get goofing around, Mike. I'm sarcastic myself, but I am learning the appropriateness of where and when I'm sarcastic and have found that sarcastic facial expressions do not fit in the bedroom. Actually, to a woman they are a major turn-off. Sarcasm at its most basic means joking by overstating the obvious, but can go much deeper than that and in the bedroom can be very insulting. At a much deeper level, sarcasm can be interpreted as intending to wound or insult and is often used as a mask for anger. It means 'the tearing of one's flesh'."

"Can't she take a joke?" Mike retorted.

"Yeah, maybe about the shirt she bought you that had a funky pattern or the way she is a neat freak . . . but not when she is lying naked in your bed," I responded.

"She gets all that from my face?" he asked.

"Maybe not *all* that from your face—but a good 90 percent or so," I responded.

Mike learned several key lessons that day about foreplay, facial expressions and communication. He now knows that only 7 percent of our communication is through words (this is a key to understanding great communication, as we discussed in the last chapter), while 93 percent of our communication is found in nonverbal displays (tone of voice, posture, eye contact, facial contortions, eyebrow movement, flared nostrils, and so on). Think about how this plays out in the bedroom. This is a key to unlocking greater sexual intimacy in your marriage.

Dealing with Insecurities

While women are often stereotyped as having body-image issues, the truth is that both men and women struggle with insecurities about their bodies.

I must admit I struggle with my body. While writing this book, I have spent some time camping with my wife's family in Minnesota—boating, fishing, the whole works. Taking my shirt off in front of family or perfect strangers fills me with anxiety. I speak in front of thousands of people a month with not an ounce of fear or trembling, but taking my shirt off in a boat with an old uncle and great-grandfather makes me cringe. It's the same struggle I had in seventh grade when the boys had to play "Skins and Shirts" in gym class. It was the quick, cheap way to distinguish members of an opposing team, but I cringed whenever I ended up on the Skins team.

Where does that fear come from? Gary has been teaching me so much about the importance of core beliefs that I have learned to spend time every day treasure hunting in my own heart. I want to know the depths of my heart by examining the messages that have been written on it. While treasure hunting, I have found some of the messages that have given me great insecurity while shirtless.

I grew up in an independent, fundamental, pre-millennial, *King James Version*-only Baptist church. My brother and I were not allowed to wear shorts, or even mow the lawn with our shirts off. When we went into public restrooms, we never used urinals. We always went into stalls. I grew up with over-the-top privacy when it came to my body.

---

*The home you grew up in determines
how you deal with your body.*

You can probably imagine the beliefs (level 6 of communication) that were in my heart when Amy and I were first married. I brought 20 years of insecurity into our marriage. At Wrigley Field, home of my beloved Chicago Cubs, the urinals in the men's restrooms are troughs 100-feet long. No walls, no dividers, no nothing—my worst nightmare!

Men's Physical Features that Create Insecurity

1. Size of penis
2. Circumcised or uncircumcised
3. Love handles
4. Acne scars
5. Too hairy
6. Tattoos

To this day, at age 33, I still purchase $100 worth of groceries I do not need just so that I can hide the condoms at the bottom of the cart. The home you grew up in determines how you deal with your body.

On our honeymoon, I actually undressed underneath the sheets or in a dark room rather than in front of my wife. That's why I'm so convinced that beliefs about our physical insecurities are essential to premarital conversations and need to be discussed prior to the wedding night.

Over the past 11 years, Amy and I have developed great security in our marriage. I feel safe with her and that has removed many of the insecurities I have about my body. Amy knows my heart beliefs. I trust her with my heart, and that brings truckloads of security into our marriage.

I believe that Solomon provides one of the best responses to the insecurities both men and women face when he says, "All beautiful you are, my darling" (4:7). For those facing body-esteem issues, Solomon's comment rings as true today as it did when he spoke it thousands of years ago. In some ways, isn't that what every man and woman wants to hear? "You are all beautiful to me!"

Solomon goes on to say, "There is no flaw in you." That's a response we each long to hear when we expose our bodies to each other.

When your wife asks how she looks in a dress, there is only one answer: "You are all beautiful to me." When he asks if his belly looks too big, there is only one answer: "You are all beautiful to me." And when she asks the granddaddy of all questions, "Do I look too fat in these jeans?" there is only one answer: "You are all beautiful to me."

Both men and women want to hear, "You are all beautiful," but it's easy to undermine that message if you get involved with pornography. I believe that pornography is as damaging to a woman as an affair. If you're a man viewing pornography, you're watching women who have more than likely been abused as children. You're watching women who probably don't eat well. You're watching women who likely had bad relationships with their fathers. You're watching women who have had plastic surgery and implants. And you're watching women who have given themselves away to an industry that couldn't care less about them. You are exposing yourself to that and getting pleasure from it. Do you know what you are telling your wife? You are telling her, "You are *not* all beautiful."

When a man goes outside of the marriage to fulfill sexual fantasies, he is shortcutting the security and intimacy in the marriage. Fulfilling sexual desires outside of the marriage brings short-lived pleasure with long-term frustration, guilt, resentment, anger and regret.

When you love your mate unconditionally, you are saying, "I love you as one who is personally autographed by God." Several things happen when you begin loving your spouse unconditionally:

• You remove the vacuum of tenderness and intimacy.
• You are no longer adversaries.

- You work at bringing pleasure to the other.
- Sex is no longer just about one person's wants and needs.
- You stay committed to the marriage.
- You communicate more freely.

Turn Off the Lights

Whenever I perform a wedding, you'll always see me talking to the groom as the bride is walking down the aisle. I'll try looking as pastoral as I possibly can before I lean over to the groom and comment, "That's as good as it gets right there." The groom usually looks at me a little confused. Then I explain, "She is going to look great today and even tonight . . . but in a few months, you're going to get used to her in a lot more comfortable, low-maintenance clothes!"

What other event besides a wedding do you begin preparing for at 5 A.M. for a 3-P.M. gathering? Every detail is micromanaged to perfection. As a result, most weddings are beautiful events—and they should be! But we can't all spend 4 to 10 hours every day getting ready.

Since Amy and I were married, I have gained 25 pounds. I know I'm not Red Lobster's fresh catch of the day, but here's what's great about it—we can still turn off the lights! With the light glow of a candle, the playing field is even. A few wrinkles, scars or even pounds disappear.

Marrying for looks is not the long-term plan. That is not the security you are looking for that is going to build intimacy. You are attracted to a person initially by looks, but a marriage does not grow and thrive based on weight, hair, muscles or smooth skin.

One of my favorite verses in the Bible is "And it came to pass." Sure, that biblical phrase has nothing to do with fleeting looks, but every time I read them, I am reminded how quickly our looks come to pass.

Solomon wrote another wonderful book called Ecclesiastes. As he brings a close to that book of wisdom, he reminds us that we all grow old and our bodies fade:

Honor and enjoy your Creator while you're still young,
Before the years take their toll and your vigor wanes,
Before your vision dims and the world blurs

And the winter years keep you close to the fire.
In old age, your body no longer serves you so well.
Muscles slacken, grip weakens, joints stiffen.
The shades are pulled down on the world.
You can't come and go at will. Things grind to a halt.
The hum of the household fades away.
You are wakened now by bird-song.
Hikes to the mountains are a thing of the past.
Even a stroll down the road has its terrors.
Your hair turns apple-blossom white,
Adorning a fragile and impotent matchstick body.
Yes, you're well on your way to eternal rest,
While your friends make plans for your funeral.
Life, lovely while it lasts, is soon over.
Life as we know it, precious and beautiful, ends.
The body is put back in the same ground it came from.
The spirit returns to God, who first breathed it
(Eccles. 12:1-7, *THE MESSAGE*).

These passages remind me of the senior woman who invited her husband upstairs to make love. After hearing her request, he told her she'd have to take her pick between those two things.

One senior lady in our church is always sharing with me the passion she and her husband share on a regular basis. She'll always say, "Ted, I could teach you young folks a thing or two about sex." She has told me that they avoid standing naked in front of mirrors because it's discouraging. And at their age, they have gotten rid of candles altogether.

Skip the French Kiss—Instead, Hebrew Kiss

Long, passionate, deep kissing during foreplay prepares your wife for sex. It communicates, "I'm ready and I want to be inside of you." Guys, don't underestimate the power of kissing in foreplay. Don't shortcut the kissing and gentle exploration of your wife's body. It goes a long way to preparing your wife for intercourse.

Solomon says, "Your lips drip sweetness as the honeycomb, my bride; milk and honey are under your tongue" (4:11). What's he doing here?

He tastes her lips and what's under her tongue. What do you call that? It's not a French kiss—it's a *Hebrew* kiss. The term "French kiss" didn't get coined until 1923, while the Hebrew kiss goes back more than 3,000 years! God invented it as part of foreplay. Solomon compares the kiss, the sweetness on his love's tongue, to honey.

A note on kissing in dating: One of the most frequently asked questions we get from those who are still dating is whether or not it is okay to kiss while dating. This verse in the Song of Songs teaches that deep French kissing is a part of foreplay and is meant to lead to the act of intercourse. And we all know the difference between a peck on the cheek—which was a common greeting among believers in New Testament times—and a deep kiss, which is reserved for married couples.

One further note, this one about kissing in general:

If you want to be happy, healthy, successful, and live longer, give your spouse a kiss before you go to work each day. That's the conclusion of a study conducted by a group of German physicians and psychologists, in cooperation with insurance companies. According to Dr. Arthur Sazbo, the study found that those who kiss their spouse each morning miss less work because of illness than those who do not. They also have fewer auto accidents on the way to work. They earn 20 to 30 percent more monthly and they live about five years more than those who don't even give each other a peck on the cheek. The reason for this, says Dr. Sazbo, is that the kissers begin the day with a positive attitude. A kiss signifies a sort of seal of approval, offer Sazbo and his colleagues, and they believe those who don't experience it, for whatever reason, go out the door feeling not quite right about themselves.[2]

Let the Fountain Flow

Women have a natural vaginal lubricant that is produced during sexual arousal or stimulation. Depending on the time of the menstrual cycle and on sexual stimulation, this vaginal lubrication will vary in color, odor and amount. In most cases, it is clear just like a man's pre-ejaculate, not the milky color of a man's ejaculate. The absence of lubrication can cause sex to be painful for the woman, and some finessing is called for if the man hopes to achieve penetration.

In Proverbs, Solomon talks about the woman's vagina and the man's genitals as a cistern and as a spring or fountain. Now in ancient times, a cistern was built to catch water during the rainy season, which was only a few months out of the whole year.

In Song of Songs, Solomon writes, "The fragrance of your garments is like that of Lebanon. You are a garden locked up, my sister, my bride; you are a spring enclosed, a sealed fountain" (4:11-12). Solomon is saying that the woman is sealed up—she's a locked fountain. In other words, she has kept herself for him alone.

As he kisses her, she begins to respond physically. He says, "Your plants are an orchard of pomegranates with choice fruits, with henna and nard, nard and saffron, calamus and cinnamon, with every kind of incense tree, with myrrh and aloes and all the finest spices" (4:13-14). Now her garden is in full bloom. He's smelling her—all of her—and enjoying her blossom.

She responds not just to what he's saying but also to how he's touching her, and he comments, "You are a garden fountain, a well of flowing water streaming down from Lebanon" (4:15). She's no longer a locked-up cistern—she's flowing freely. Natural lubrication is flowing down her legs. She is at the peak of sexual arousal. Desire and foreplay have moved her there.

This is a portrait of holy hot sex in the Bible. Sometimes I just sit in awe of the genius behind making love. In a single act, I can pour out my emotions and feelings and with a little touch bring my wife to great pleasure and express to her what's in my heart for her. God designed couples to have vibrant sex lives. Not only is it biblical—it's part of God's plan.

Now what's interesting is that the focus of the text is on the woman—not the man. All the sexual energy is being poured into the woman and making her feel honored, secure, beautiful and aroused. At this point, she is so turned on that she's just flowing. She opens herself up to him. She wants him badly, so badly, she cries out, "Awake, north wind, and come, south wind!" She's saying, "Be strong with me—take me!"

Look again at what Solomon has done: He's prepared for this moment all day. He's made the day special for her. He's loved on her. He's affirmed her. He prepared the room. He approaches her gently.

And she responds. (It's more than just okay for women to make sounds during sex; both partners should talk and affirm each other during intercourse, and let each other know what's pleasurable.)

Expect the Sex to Keep Getting Better

I've been married now for 11 years, and I've told you that sex gets better with time. I'm more in love and crazier about Amy today than I was 12 years ago when I met her. Honor and security—as we discussed in chapters 2 and 3—have been foundational in the growth of our relationship.

But in regard to intimacy, there have been plenty of times over the past couple of years when I have barely made it to intercourse. Amy and I have so enjoyed each other prior to sex that I am almost done before we even get to the "big act." I used to be embarrassed by that, but Amy and I have both reached the conclusion that it is okay. We want oneness and connection more than an orgasm. Notice that I did not say we do not want orgasm. We do. It has just been lowered on our priority list. We crave oneness and connection more. We can even have foreplay without the sex.

The world is trying to feed us this belief that true studs can go forever in intercourse before orgasm or climax. I want to challenge that thinking! I think a true stud knows and practices great foreplay, starting early in the morning. There may be times when you or your spouse will be done with intercourse within a minute or two of penetration. Most probably, such times will follow sessions of intense, prolonged foreplay.

The greater the intensity and longevity of foreplay, the quicker the orgasm. If a husband penetrates his wife with no foreplay, he will obviously go a lot longer—especially if his last ejaculation was only a day or so ago. Guys, have you ever been frustrated with how long it takes to get your wife there? The secret to getting your wife to orgasm is found in foreplay. And foreplay is not always what happens 30 minutes prior to sex. Great foreplay begins early in the morning. Emotional connection is foreplay to your wife. Domestic support is foreplay to your wife.

In the next chapter, we'll talk about the real ins and outs of sex—all the things Dan's high-school buddies never told him.

From GarySmalley.com

Q: I know I'm supposed to love my spouse unconditionally, but he is so annoying. He doesn't wear cologne, so he stinks a lot of the time. He makes weird noises that turn me off. Honestly, I'm no longer attracted to him physically. I hate sex. I'm only tolerating him and staying in the relationship because he's faithful to me and God's Word says I have no grounds for divorce. Please help!

A: If we expect our mate to be the source of our happiness, we are sure to be disappointed in the long run.

Success in marriage is not defined as two people staying together for a lifetime. For that matter, a monogamous marriage is not enough. *We define success as two people thrilled about the marriage.*

Physical attraction may have brought you and your husband together, but as time goes by, I guarantee it will not keep you together. Physical attraction is not the key ingredient to faithfulness.

When coming face to face with inevitable disappointment, many people assume they must have married the wrong person. Some may resort to an affair to recharge their battery. The stolen charge may light up the circuits for a moment, but after the glow fades, they will feel emptier and more miserable than before. Even if they divorce and remarry the "right person," they will encounter the same frustration. The problem is not in the person they marry; it is in their expectations that that person will make them happy and keep them charged day after day. Wrong.

Sooner or later we run headlong into an inescapable fact: No person on earth is capable of giving us the fulfillment we crave. We can never plug into enough people to keep our lives filled with the happiness we want. It's no wonder so many people consider suicide as a way out. By depending on people to make us happy, we not only miss the positive emotions we crave, but we also saddle ourselves with the very negative emotions we want to avoid—deep frustration, disappointment, hurt feelings, worry, anxiety, fear, unrest, uncertainty and confusion. These emotions are the inevitable result of depending on a person, place or thing for fulfillment. The bottom line? We're just not wired to plug into other people as our power source.

Have you expressed your desire for him to smell a little better or for the noises to be taken to the bathroom? A husband who is creating security for his wife would have the desire to avoid obnoxious behavior.

Do you pray for your husband? I've always found it difficult to harbor bitterness toward someone that I am fervently seeking God's best for in prayer. Praying for someone helps me to see that person through the lens of Christ. I want to see my spouse as Christ does.

We want to validate the fact that your husband's annoying habits are frustrating. But remember the power of confirmation bias. When you make the decision in your heart that your husband is annoying, you only look for behaviors that support that decision. When you choose to honor and esteem him as highly valuable to Jesus, you will begin to see behaviors that show his value. Then you are on your way to creating security in your marriage.

My prayer for you is that your marriage will move from tolerable to good and then from good to great!

Notes

1. Louann Brizendine, M.D., *The Female Brain* (New York: Morgan Road Books, 2007), p. 15.
2. "Kissing," *Bits and Pieces* (July 25, 1992), pp. 4-5, quoted at *Bible.org*, 2007. http://www.bible.org/illus.php?topic_id=860 (accessed August 24, 2007).

Summary

It can be as exciting and pleasurable for wives
to connect with their husbands emotionally
as it is sexually.

For women, foreplay starts early in the morning.
Men are ready most anytime.

Great foreplay begins long before couples actually
touch and continues once they do. It begins with the
words they speak to one another.

The top thing a woman wants from a man is
gentleness. The top thing a man wants from a
woman is *responsiveness*.

Pillow Talk

Can you give me two or three ideas for foreplay?
What gets you in the mood more than anything?

What are some practical ways we can prepare
the bedroom for lovemaking?

When you see my face throughout the day, what does it
communicate? Do I respond to you the way you enjoy?

What parts of your body are you insecure about?
What can I do to ease those insecurities?

CHAPTER 8

The Three Big Sexpectations

You cannot read a book by two authors from Branson, Missouri, without getting a little country music. We are surrounded by it in our little town in the Ozarks. Several years back, the husband and wife team of Tim McGraw and Faith Hill sang a wonderful song, "Let's Make Love," about their desire for physical union (which sounds a lot like Solomon when he was invited to enjoy lovemaking all through the night until daybreak):

Until the sun comes up, let's make love.

The desire to make love all night long versus the actual ability to do so was quite a surprise to me (Ted) on my honeymoon. Amy and I were married in October in her hometown of Fremont, Nebraska. It felt more like a family reunion than it did a wedding. All of my family was in from Chicago. All of Amy's family was in from Minnesota. The weekend schedule went as follows:

Friday
Flew in from Georgia where I was serving on staff at a church
Met Amy at church to practice song I was singing at wedding
Went to hotel to meet my family and friends
6 P.M. Rehearsal
7:30 P.M. Rehearsal dinner
8:00 P.M. to 11:00 P.M. Men's night out (Bowling)

Saturday

7:00 A.M. to 11:00 A.M. Golfing with the groomsmen

1:00 P.M. Pictures

2:00 P.M. Wedding

3:00 P.M. More pictures

5:00 P.M. Reception

11:00 P.M. Check-in at hotel for passionate night

Yeah, right!

We had a 6:45 A.M. flight to catch the next morning. We love our families, but being the center of attention for two days can get tiring. Our first night did not meet our expectations. Amy planned on passion and romance. I planned on endurance. Our expectations went unmet.

For those reading this book who are planning on having sex for six-plus hours on their honeymoon, I want to share an ancient Hebrew phrase for you: "Ain't gonna happen!" (Okay, that's not actually an ancient Hebrew phrase, but there's so much truth there that it ought to be.)

Before we get into the expectations we all bring to the bedroom, however, it is important for us to restate the central theme of this book: *The quality of your marital relationship is far more important than the quality of your sex.* Trying a new sexual position, going with quickies or adding music will not fix your marriage. Honor, security and intimacy come before sex.

The Gap Between Expectations and Reality

We have expectations about everything: what time our mate gets home from work, the safest speed for driving, the spending of money, the raising of kids and the type of church we should attend—all subjects that can drain and strain a relationship.

One of the biggest energy-draining experiences most adults stumble through is a strained marriage. I (Gary) think back over the number of times Norma and I have been bent out of shape over different expectations in any and every area of life. It's amazing how the tone of our relationship could get so dark so fast.

Your strained marriage relationship is like a circle. The strain can start with a disappointment over one of your expectations, and then, before you know it, your desire for sex declines—and that may disappoint one or both of you. Relationship and the reality of sex go hand in hand.

The gap between what we expect sexually and what we get can also drain our energy. When our experience is close to what we anticipated, we're stronger and more content. That bolsters our ability to keep on loving. But unless we talk about those things and bring our expectations to the surface, our wishes won't be known for sure, and we may find ourselves facing an energy-sapping gap between our desires and our reality.

Are your expectations realistic and healthy? Are you willing to sit down and share your expectations with your spouse? Are you open to listening to each other and learning new, more pragmatic expectations for each other?

We all have expectations regarding sex. We get them from actors following scripts, musicians tugging at our heartstrings and friends exaggerating their experiences. And when churches and parents go silent, we get our education elsewhere. Unfortunately, that education is not always correct, and that fact coupled with our unvoiced expectations can lead to a lot of stress and frustration.

Any time you experience stress or frustration—whether it's at home, at work or in your sex life—the root cause is the same: the gap between your expectations and reality. It looks like this:

Your Expectations ←THE GAP→ Reality

The gap is your level of stress and frustration. The greater the gap, the greater level of stress you have. There could be a significant gap, thus significant stress and frustration, or your gap could be relatively small. For example, if you planned on sex twice a month and only had sex once a month, your stress and frustration would be lower than if you got no sex at all. In this chapter we're going to examine the three big sexpectations and how you can close the gap between your expectations and reality. Your love life won't be the same.

The size of your gap depends on the three common expectations about the act of intercourse that we all bring into our marriage. We call them *sexpectations*: The Frequency Sexpectation (how often you and your spouse have sex), The Endurance Sexpectation (how long lovemaking will last each time) and The Performance Sexpectation (how your lover will perform).

The Three Sexpectations

The Frequency Sexpectation
(how often you'll have sex)

The Endurance Sexpectation
(how long lovemaking will last)

The Performance Sexpectation
(how your lover will perform)

The Frequency Sexpectation

The Frequency Sexpectation is an issue for almost every married couple, and many couples become frustrated when this sexpectation is not met.

3 or 4 Times a Week ← THE GAP → Once a Month

How often should a couple have sex? Frequency varies with age, stage in life and number of years married. When I (Ted) got married, I was handed a box that was beautifully gold-wrapped with a slit in the top. When I asked what the empty box was for, I was told to put a dollar in the box every time Amy and I made love in the first two years of marriage. Then after year two, I should take a dollar out every time we made love. That way I would always have plenty of emergency money handy throughout my lifetime. What made matters worse was that it was my mother-in-law who gave me the box. I'm thrilled to report that my mother-in-law, while right most of the time, was wrong on this one: Amy and I make love as often now as we did when we were first married. But I must admit that between our fourth and seventh anniversaries, we slowed down a bit. This is not uncommon, but it can be avoided.

If you are in a marriage right now in which lovemaking is seldom rather than often, there is hope. You can change. Your lovemaking frequency can change, but it does not start in the bedroom. It starts with security.

One Hundred Days of Sex

People will go to all kinds of extremes to spice up their sex life and increase the frequency of their sex. Doug and Annie Brown felt as though their sexual intimacy was growing stagnant, so they decided to increase the frequency of the sex in their marriage—and they made the national news: They made it their mission to have sex every day for 100 days.

Gary Stollman, a relationship expert based in Beverly Hills, California, made the following observation about the couple's efforts:

> Problems with sex are usually the symptom of a relationship gone bad, not the cause, and I wouldn't say sex on its own is the answer. The act of consciously putting in daily energy into a relationship is essential to its vitality and longevity and this has to be done on all levels, not just the sexual. In theory, the gist of what they're trying to do—put effort into the relationship—is absolutely what needs to be done. I look at it as a metaphor. One hundred days of straight sex is not necessarily going to fix things but it is a great metaphor for putting the energy back into a relationship.[1]

What this couple should have done is work on improving their listening skills, increasing their honor for each other, and building in more security. The best thing you can do is stop trying to improve your mate and make a list of what you should work on to improve yourself. You should also find sections of Scripture that correspond to your areas of need and brand these living, powerful Scriptures into your heart by memorizing them and meditating upon them day and night until they reach your heart. That's when you'll see major changes in your life, and that is what will improve your sex life.

Addressing Frequency Sexpectations

Amy and I had to work through The Frequency Sexpectation, and I am thrilled to report that the outcome is great.

One reason the frequency of sex has increased in our marriage is because I have started to initiate sex a lot more. For the first six or seven years of our marriage, Amy initiated sex 9 out of 10 times. You may be thinking, *What's wrong with you, Ted? Are you a normal man?*

I must take you back to my independent, fundamental, *King James Version*-only upbringing. Sex was a shamed-based teaching while I was growing up. I was not equipped to deal with or think properly about sex. The belief that started to be developed in my heart was subtle. For some reason I felt like a pervert when I initiated sex with my wife. I know that sounds weird, but deep down I didn't want Amy to be in on the little secret that I thought about sex a lot. As a result, we were not having sex as often as I would have preferred. I lived with a low level of frustration brought on by my having to constantly wonder, *Is tonight the night?*

I need to point out that in my mind, this is not all that bad. It's part of growing together as a couple. Learning every last cue, preference and desire of your spouse can't happen in the first five years of marriage. Such education takes a lifetime. It is a journey. That is why you cannot give up on sex—or your marriage for that matter—too early.

It was just four years ago that the frequency of sex changed in our marriage. And there were two main factors that made the difference: Amy's gentle confrontation and her understanding. Through her personal studying and spiritual journey, she learned that I think about sex a lot more than her. That understanding of the male brain led to an increase in our frequency of sex.

Amy also confronted the underlying truth of our marriage in a very gentle way: She was the primary initiator.

"You know I initiate 9 out of 10 times, don't you?" She said in our seventh year of marriage.

"Yeah," was the best answer I could muster. After all, she was right.

That night we talked for hours about our hearts. We learned things about each other that we couldn't have learned any other way. She saw more of my fundamentalist upbringing and how it drastically affected our love life. She recognized that I was still attracted to her in a big way. She did something that night that changed our marriage forever. She gave me permission to request sex anytime. Now, that does not mean that I take her in the kitchen somewhere between serving Carson macaroni and cheese and loading the dishwasher. I follow the teaching from the first six chapters in this book: Creating honor and security in our marriage is still the priority.

Today, Amy and I share the initiation. Neither of us lives with the frustration of wondering if tonight is the night.

There are many ways a couple can resolve the frequency sexpectation and here are a few:

1. *Set times and places.* Be cautious to not allow routine to turn into a rut. (We'll address this more in the next chapter.)
2. *Develop your own code.* One of the elders at our church recently shared with me the code he and wife share on the nights they are preparing for sex. They use the phrase "working on the budget" to share their intentions. Their goal is to use that term as many times as they can in front of their kids. To date, even their 12-year-old has not caught on to the real meaning of the phrase.
3. *Share the initiation.*
4. *Set your alarm clock 10 minutes early for a quickie.*
5. *Offer grace to each other.* When the "Tonight's the Night" doesn't work out, do not get angry.
6. *Have a certain candle that when lit means that it's time for sex.* The kids will never figure this one out.
7. *Plan family weekends away.* There's nothing like going to a bed and breakfast and waiting for the kids to fall asleep.
8. *Rent a motor home for the weekend.* It's great for the relationship with the entire family and it provides variety. (Just make

sure everyone forgives each other on the way home Sunday afternoon.)

9. *Respect each other's right to be him- or herself, and respect what each one likes to do before sex.* For example, some women do not like talking about the "special night" in a joking way during the same day.

The Endurance Sexpectation

The Endurance Sexpectation concerns how long lovemaking will last. That means we need to address two words men hate: "premature ejaculation." Whether they can admit it or not, every man I know has struggled with this aspect of sex.

All Night   ← **THE GAP** →   10 Minutes

Men struggle with ejaculatory control. We hit a certain point that I call "the point of no return," and we have no control. It's going to happen. Ejaculatory control can even turn into a disorder for some men.

Premature ejaculation (PE), also known as rapid ejaculation, premature climax, early ejaculation, or by the Latin term *ejaculatio praecox,* is the most common sexual problem in men, affecting 25%-40% of men. It is characterized by a lack of voluntary control over ejaculation. Masters and Johnson stated that a man suffers from premature ejaculation if he ejaculates before his partner achieves orgasm in more than fifty percent of his sexual encounters. Other sex researchers have defined premature ejaculation as occurring if the man ejaculates within two minutes or less of penetration; however, a survey by Alfred Kinsey in the 1950s demonstrated that three quarters of men ejaculated within two minutes of penetration in over half of their sexual encounters. Today, most sex therapists understand premature ejaculation as occurring when a lack of ejaculatory control interferes with sexual or emotional well-being in one or both partners. Most men experience premature ejaculation at least once in their lives. Often adolescents and young men experience "premature" ejaculation during their first sexual encounters, but eventually learn ejaculatory control.[2]

Ejaculatory control tends to increase with age. In the process of writing this book, I have been asking men in my small group and in our church how long they can go before orgasm. I have asked men from 20 to 80 years old, and here are some of their responses:

"I make it my goal to make sure she gets there several times before I do." —60-year-old

"I can go until she gets there and then I get there too." —49-year-old

"It seems as though she never gets there." —25-year-old newlywed

A group of gals were asked the same question by my wife. Here were the responses:

"How do you know you have reached orgasm?" —26-year-old, married for three years

"Do we both need to get there at the same time?" —23-year-old, soon-to-be married

"The pace of my day, stress at work and unwinding activities at night are all variables in whether or not I get there. They are also variables in how long it takes. Women have so many variables." —40-year-old, married for 15 years

For years in our marriage, I struggled with performance expectations. Not only did I want to last a long time, but I also wanted to guarantee that my wife experienced an orgasm. I can admit to you (with

Amy's permission) that early in our marriage, I ended most of our love-making with an apology: "Amy, I'm sorry. I held out as long as I could. I thought about everything from the State of the Union Address to grilling burgers and nothing worked. I got there before you."

"Would you stop that, Ted," Amy would argue. "It doesn't always have to be about me."

"I know, but I want to pleasure you as much as you want to pleasure me," I argued.

What a way to end a day of romance, intimacy and sex. I was a fool.

Sex Drives

God created sex drives, and men usually have different sex drives than women. For instance, men tend to use sex as a stress reliever, whereas women lose libido with stress. Just as Solomon desired sex with his new bride after a long day at work, men view sex as a vacation. Women tend to view sex as something that takes their energy rather than infusing them with energy.

In some cases, a guy may not understand why his wife is not responsive. I am amazed at the number of women who have confessed in my office to their husband for the first time, after years of marriage, that they were abused as a child. The husband never knew why there was this big wall down the middle of their bed. Sex is rarely the core issue in a marriage, so if things aren't quite right in bed, then it's worth treasure hunting to discover what else might be going on.

On the other hand, I must admit, on behalf of men worldwide, we at times must fight low-level jealousy over the fact that women can achieve multiple orgasms. Please do not get me wrong: I thoroughly enjoy climax, but at times I think it is amazing that God has created women to achieve a climax more than once in one lovemaking session.

Women also have more control over their orgasms than men do. Men can work through distractions during sex and still reach orgasm. A woman, on the other hand, hears a peep on the baby monitor and she's done. I can't tell you the number of times the baby monitor has turned our all-day romance and evening of passion into a quickie for me. I curse the day the inventor of the baby monitor was born.

Skills for Prolonging Orgasm

While premature ejaculation is defined as a medical disorder, prolonging orgasm for men is a learned skill. There are no set medical standards for how long it should take a man, or a woman, to reach orgasm; and the length of time will differ according to energy level, distractions, hormones and foreplay involved. There are, however, a few techniques to try to avoid premature ejaculation.

The Start-and-Stop Method

I call the start-and-stop method of prolonging orgasm "passing the threshold." One way to prolong orgasm is to go right to the threshold but not walk through it. Stop at the doorway. Give yourself a breather, much like you do when you stop while working to wipe the sweat from your brow. Then when you have relaxed for a moment, you can continue. The hard part is getting comfortable expressing the threshold to your wife in the middle of lovemaking.

How do I do that? Glad you asked. *Tell her.* "Hold on." "Give me a second." "Wait." Use whatever language works for you.

Minimal Foreplay

Keep foreplay to a minimum. I know we just spent the entire previous chapter encouraging foreplay and teaching on it—but prolonged foreplay can decrease endurance.

Condoms

You can start with the start-and-stop method and add the condom after the first or second threshold. Condoms come in varying degrees of sensitivity. You may need to experiment a little with different brands to find the perfect condom for your rhythm and lovemaking.

Energy

Sex takes energy. And sex is worth saving some of your energy for. That is part of preparing yourself for your mate.

We all have a daily allotment of energy. I like to call them bursts of energy. Energy is based on a number of variables: job, diet, exercise, health, sickness, disabilities, kids and home. One key to your love life with your mate is to figure out how many bursts you have in a typical day. Most people have a few bursts of energy each day, though I don't think I know anyone who has more than ten. For instance, I have about three or four bursts of energy in a day. I know when I have used one and what it will take to get prepared for the next. Quiet time, reading, praying, resting, napping and sleeping are just a few of the ways to get reenergized.

Here's why this is important: No matter how many bursts of energy you have on a typical day, always save at least one burst for your mate. If you know you must lead the staff meeting at 10 A.M., know that you will use a burst of energy. If you are coaching your kids' soccer game later that night, you'll need a burst of energy for that as well. You control your bursts of energy and no one else, so save some for sex. If you approach your lovemaking with low energy, the chances are higher that orgasm will happen more quickly.

The Performance Sexpectation

What moves does your mate have? Can your mate contort his or her body like an Olympic gymnast? Does your mate scream and pant? Does your wife act like Meg Ryan in the film *When Harry Met Sally*? Does your mate bring out the tiger in you?

If Hollywood has ever fed us a load of junk, it's in the realm of performance sexpectations. Take a stroll through the local bookstore's magazine aisle and you will see an array of performance-centered headlines scream from the front pages:

"Make Him Crazy in Bed!"
"Know His Hot Spots!"
"6 Secrets to Make Him *Beg* for More"
"The Sex Moves You've Never Heard of Before"

There's a cultural obsession with performance. We want to bat a thousand in bed. But I can tell you that I've had plenty of poor performances when it comes to my sex life—and I've learned from all of them.

Loud and Contorting	←THE GAP→	Quiet and Still

Just this past week, I discovered something new about my wife: She cannot be romanced while camping.

We've already learned that women are all-day lovers. The emotional connection needs to start early in the morning, and nonsexual touches need to be delivered throughout the day. Lovingly listening to each other while together; helping with the kids, housework and various chores; learning new things together: These and a host of other activities prepare a woman for sex. Distractions must be removed. Domestic support needs to be provided. The bedroom must be prepared. None of that happened on our camping trip to Minnesota.

We had reserved a two-bedroom fishing cabin and planned to spend the week camping with Amy's family. While I enjoy spending time with family, breaking our regular routine and attempting to coordinate the schedules of 20 people can be exhausting. We had a bedroom for Corynn and a bedroom for Carson. Amy and I opted to take the pull-out couch in the main living area of the cabin. The entire cabin shared a one-window air-conditioning unit, which kept the inside of the cabin at 80 degrees—even at 10 P.M. (Remember that my wife knows when the thermostat is set on 70 or 71 degrees at home. One degree makes a difference for her.)

As we lay in bed our first night, we began romancing each other—until we discovered that we could feel every spring the bed had to offer. The full-sized mattress was so uncomfortable that we decided to sleep parallel to the back of the couch. With the heat, the uncomfortable bed and the dingy floor, I knew we weren't going to be having sex anytime soon. All we could do was laugh and be thankful that the kids were comfortable.

As far as my performance, I'd give myself a D-minus, but that's being generous. After driving a minivan with six people in it for 11 hours, I was too tired to prepare the room—and there wasn't much of a room to prepare. Distractions were everywhere. And did I mention that the walls were paper thin?

But do you know what? Throughout that whole week of heat, poor sleeping conditions and family, Amy and I flirted like crazy. We had fun with it. I never laughed more about poor performance or missed opportunities in my 11 years of marriage to her. It taught us a great lesson about freedom and flexibility. We could go the week without sex and still be great. It made me anticipate the trip home. We actually cut that vacation short by a day and a half. I was less than truthful with the family as to why we were leaving. There was no way I was going to tell Amy's side of the family that I wanted to get home to have sex. (Of course, now they know.)

You have two choices when it comes to The Performance Sexpectation: (1) You can become frustrated with unmet expectations and grow cold toward your mate and lovemaking, or (2) You can start talking with your mate. Chances are, your husband or wife does not even know some of your desires. Start talking. Here are some discussion jump starters to get you going on your journey to mutually satisfying sex:

- What position is most comfortable for you?
- Do you prefer to be on top or on bottom?
- Am I too rough when I kiss or massage your breasts?
- Is there anything I ever do that makes you uncomfortable or causes you pain?
- I enjoy having sex ___ times per week or month.
- I like it best when you . . . (share it all, even if after a few years the list is five pages long).
- It makes me uncomfortable when you . . .

When to Seek Help

Several years ago, I was contacted by a dear family friend who wanted out of his marriage. I told him to meet me for coffee, and I would do everything I could to help.

After we ordered our coffee, he wasted no time in telling me that he and his wife had not had sex in more than two years. I knew their daughter was not quite two years old, and I could do the math. Because

I was only meeting with him, I kept the focus on what he was doing and what he could do differently. We did not deal with any of his wife's issues—just his.

He started with, "She still has the baby weight and is exhausted from being a new mom."

"Since she is not here to speak for herself," I said, "let's focus on you and your responsibility. What are your expectations of your wife?"

He was struggling with all three sexpectations. "I want to have sex a couple of times a week. I want her to want me like she did when we first met." I pointed out to him that getting their relationship back to where it was when they first married would be easier than he might think.

My friend started working on the marriage, not the sex. He started laying the foundations of honor and security, and the frequency of their sex increased. He did not work on the marriage to increase the frequency. That goes back to the female radar we talked about earlier. He truly wanted to rediscover the love they had once had. Over time, the sex they once had returned, and it was a glorious by-product of the nurturing.

There are many variables in the bedroom, and while most sexual struggles between couples are relational, there are times when the problem is medical. Here are just a few reasons you should seek help from medical doctors and professional therapists:

- Impotence
- Urinating during orgasm (affects some 5 percent of women)
- Pain during intercourse
- Prolonged menstrual cycles
- Prolonged erections
- Depression
- Sexually transmitted disease (STD)
- Sexual abuse experienced in childhood or a previous marriage
- Infertility

I spend much of my time as a pastor counseling, and I am very comfortable answering and working through most questions and situations with a couple. Yet I know my limits. I know what I have been trained to do, and I stick close to it. Because I care deeply for the congregation that God has entrusted to me, I refer individuals to professional help when appropriate. Your pastor may be a good person to ask for a name when you're seeking professional help, or when you want to check the integrity of something a therapist or doctor has suggested. I have worked with couples who have had a therapist tell them to view pornography together to spice it up; I've also worked with couples trying to get pregnant who were counseled to harvest multiple eggs to produce multiple zygotes.

Countless times at church and at seminars after speaking on sex, I've had couples approach me and say, "We wish we would have learned those lessons 20 years ago." Don't wait too long to ask the right questions.

Now that you know the three biggest sexpectations and are ready to close the gap between your expectations and reality, it's time to turn up the heat and discover how to cultivate creativity in the bedroom.

From GarySmalley.com

Q: I am a sexual addict. It has taken me forever to get to the point where I can admit that. I know my struggle with lust is destroying my marriage. What can I do?

A: Lust makes us think that having some person we don't presently have would make us happier. Often that person is simply a figment of our imagination.

Even if the person is real, we often attach character traits to him or her that are not real. Usually our lust focuses on sexual involvement. We imagine someone who is terribly fond of us and who prefers our presence and intimacy over anyone else's. We imagine that if we had such a person to hold in our arms, it would be exciting and wonderfully fulfilling. This is a terrible deception, for we forget or ignore the devastating consequences of living out our imaginations.

Sensual dreams reveal our selfish desire for stimulation. Unchecked, sensual stimulation actually increases the desire. We see this exhibited in several ways. For example, one of the primary reasons people smoke or consume alcohol or drugs is to stimulate their physical senses. As a person continues in this selfish frame of mind, the desire grows until he or she needs regular and increasing doses of stimulation.

First, recognize the basic motive behind this emotion. Lust is not serving a person in love; it is viewing a person as an object to be used.

Second, lust can reconfirm our awareness that God, not another's body—not even our mate's—is the source of our fulfillment. As pleasurable as sex can be, it can never substitute for the lasting joy and satisfaction of knowing God.

Third, in the midst of lustful thoughts, as an act of our will, we can pray something like this: "Lord, I know there are times when I wish my mate acted sexier. And there are even times I have entertained thoughts about being in the arms of another person. All the advertisements on TV have tried to convince me it would be exciting. But right here and now, I continue to trust You to energize my life and provide all I need. I am willing to rest and wait in Your faithfulness."

You can overcome sexual addiction by God's grace and by hiding His wonderful, alive and powerful words within your heart. For example, memorize Galatians 5:13. Most likely, though, you cannot do it alone. Join a small group of people struggling with sex issues. Listen to their stories of victory and defeat. Let their stories encourage you. We have found that the greatest channel through which addicts recover is the help and support of others. Choose a group that you trust. Choose a group that will not judge you but that will help you overcome what so many people struggle with on a daily basis. God changes lives through His Word and through relationships.

Notes

1. Nick Hazell, "Finding Love Again with 100 Days of Sex: Career-Focused Couple's Radical Attempt to Revive Relationship," *ABC News,* June 1, 2007. http://abcnews.go.com/US/story?id=323072 (accessed August 2007).

2. "Premature Ejaculation," *Wikipedia, the Free Encyclopedia,* August 26, 2007. http://en.wikipedia.org/wiki/Premature_ejaculation (accessed August 2007).

Summary

The gap between what we expect sexually and
what we get can strain a marriage.

The gap is our level of stress and frustration.
The greater the gap, the greater level of stress we have.

The Frequency Sexpectation answers the
question, "How often should a couple have sex?"
Frequency varies with age, stage in life and
number of years married.

The Endurance Sexpectation concerns how
long lovemaking will last.

The Performance Sexpectation evaluates the
moves, expressions and actions of your mate
during lovemaking.

Pillow Talk

What position is most comfortable for you?
Do you prefer to be on top or on bottom?

Am I too rough when I kiss or massage
your breasts and/or genitals?

Is there anything I ever do that makes you
uncomfortable or causes you pain?

I enjoy having sex _____ times per week or month.

CHAPTER 9

Cultivate Creativity

A pastor from Memphis went golfing at Memphis National Golf Club a few weeks ago. He was even par through the seventeenth hole. He ended up double bogeying that hole and went on to par the eighteenth. He was mad and frustrated that the seventeenth hole kept him from parring the course.

Later that night, he shared with his wife his intense pain and frustration over his round. Not being much into golf or the male drive for competition or sports, she comforted him the best she could.

A week later they went on a date. At the end of the date, late into the evening, she pulled into the Memphis National Golf Club.

"What are we doing here?" the pastor asked.

"Take me to the seventeenth hole," she replied.

"Why?"

"Just take me there. I want to see this hole that has caused you such pain," she insisted.

Moments later, in the black of night, the couple arrived at the seventeenth hole.

"I want to make sure that you only have good memories of the seventeenth hole," she said.

Can you guess how the story ends? Yep, you are right.

Now that pastor's favorite playing green in the whole world is at the seventeenth hole at Memphis National Golf Club.

My (Ted's) most creative night with Amy was on our seventh wedding anniversary. I took Amy to Big Cedar, a swanky resort in Branson. It's decorated in a rustic outdoor theme. Complete with stained glass, floor-to-ceiling stone fireplaces and exposed wooden beams, the private log cabins are unforgettable.

Due to our financial situation, I could only afford one night, but I wanted it to be the best ever. I had candles, lotion, flowers and a half cord of wood for the fireplace ready to go. (Do you remember earlier when I challenged you to install a fireplace in your bedroom? If that's not a possibility where you live, then at least rent a room with one every few years. There's nothing like the flicker of a fire and the snapping of cured oak to spice up a romantic evening.) Meanwhile, the Jacuzzi was filled with warm water and inviting bubbles. This was not going to be any ordinary night of making love.

We had just finished dinner, and I knew the room was ready to go. We returned to our cabin for our evening together. Without going into too much detail, we were about 10 minutes into our intimacy when we heard a knock at the door.

"What's that?" Amy asked.

"Somebody's at the door," I answered, apprehensively noticing that the door was only about four feet from the bed and we were only separated from our visitor by a sheer fabric curtain and a panel of glass.

"What do we do?"

"Nothing—I'm sure they'll go away," I said hopefully.

"Do you think they heard us?" Amy asked sheepishly.

"Keep your voice down," I whispered. "They can't know we're in here!"

The person knocked again. Then we heard the clicking of a key being inserted into the door.

"Nooo!" I shouted. "We're in here!" The door opened halfway before I could get the words out of my mouth.

For seven years we had managed to keep it a secret that Pastor Ted and his wife, Amy, had sex. We were convinced that no one knew—well, except for the fact that we had kids. Now the secret was out. The candles, the roaring fireplace, the scent of lotion—there was no denying it!

At the time, my friend Tony was the general manager of the resort. I still haven't forgiven him for authorizing turndown service that night. In embarrassment, I decided to take advantage of the automatic checkout the next morning. I was mortified at the thought of hearing a staff member say, "That's the guy from cabin 412—I think he's a pastor!"

Amy and I still laugh about that evening together. We didn't allow that incident to stop us from pursuing creativity and pleasure on that night, or on nights that have followed. Cultivating creativity in the bedroom is a pleasure in itself; and in this chapter, you're going to discover how to do so in your own bedroom: You're going to discover practical ways to become an all-day lover.

The Importance of Breaking Routine

I'm encouraged when I meet couples who are not afraid to explore each other with creative sexual methods and settings. Breaking routine is healthy for your sexual intimacy. I am even more encouraged when I hear stories of senior couples who still like to mess around. One senior woman recently told me:

> We didn't see each other naked for the first three months of marriage. There weren't any lights or candles. We started with only straight intercourse—no foreplay. By year five, we were using candles and messing around for maybe 15 minutes prior to sex. It wasn't until year eight that we started talking about sex—what we each liked and disliked. By year ten, we started having sex in other parts of the house. Prior to that, it was only in the bedroom. It wasn't until our fifteenth wedding anniversary that I asked him if he would like me to experiment with other positions. It was sometime in this period that I had my first multiple orgasm. We enjoyed great sex for the next 35 years. He was 70 when a medical procedure put an end to sex, but it didn't end our lovemaking. I can still remember our last time. We both cried as if we were mourning a death. But you know what? We can still mess around!

Not only is this an encouraging word from a great, godly woman, it's also from a woman who is convinced that I will never be able to teach her a thing about sex! She inspires me to pursue greatness in my marriage and love life with Amy.

A lot of Christians get uncomfortable when we try to combine the words "creative" and "sex." However, I believe that God wants us to cultivate creativity in our sex lives. God only speaks to Solomon and the Shulammite bride in a single verse in the Song of Songs—immediately following intercourse:

Eat, O friends, and drink; drink your fill, O lovers (Song of Songs 5:1).

We are creatures of habit. I know I'm prone to live every part of my life like the sign found on a rugged Alaskan highway: "Choose your rut carefully; you'll be in it for the next 200 miles." But let's be frank: A rut is nothing more than a grave with both ends knocked out. Predictable and familiar, ruts offer us false security and can drain the life right out of a marriage. I'm a guy that can eat Cheerios every morning for three years straight. I never ask for menus at familiar restaurants, because I always get the same thing. Yet I pastor a church with the motto, *Never do the same thing twice.* You'll never see a drama or a video or hear a message more than once at our church. We spend countless hours a week keeping it fresh. This creativity takes a whole lot of work, but the payoff is huge. We believe that creativity and excellence honor God and inspire people.

Creativity in your marriage takes a whole lot of work, but the payoff is huge.

If this is true in the Church, how much more is it true in our lives? Creativity in your marriage also takes a whole lot of work, but the payoff is huge. Ever wonder where the romance went? Ever seem like you are drifting? That loss of romance and that drifting are the result of ruts. The reason the romance seemed so exciting at first is because it was new and fresh. Dr. Gary Chapman, marriage and family-life expert, calls it "the tingles." Remember when you had the tingles for your wife? Remember when you couldn't get enough of your husband? Ever want to get those days back? Guess what? You can! And we want to show you how.

The answer is creativity.

Key Caution

You'll notice that this chapter about creativity is not near the front of the book. That's on purpose. The foundation of honor, security and intimacy is the bedrock on which to build creativity. One reason affairs get started is because individuals are looking for "greener grass." Greener grass deceives you into believing that you must go outside of the marriage to experience greater heights of sexual intimacy, without all the responsibility. That's simply not true.

Now, whenever people combine the words "creativity" and "sex," a lot of minds run toward the words "kinky" and "perverse." But that's not the case at all! Creativity is healthy and may be just what your humdrum sex life is looking for. The best part is that you can enjoy it guilt-free and with greater passion than ever.

The All-Day Male Lover

While most men are ready for sex all day, it often takes all day for a woman to be ready for sex. Ladies cook slowly, taking their time. If your bedroom feels like there is a barbed-wire fence going down the center of it, then you need to realize that while guys are turned on by what they see, women are turned on by what they are feeling emotionally.

Ask your wife if she would mind sharing with you everything and anything that you can do for her or say to her during a typical day in order to strengthen your loving relationship. She may mention better communication. If so, ask her to expand on this topic, because you can never learn too much. She may ask for more gentle and affectionate touching. If so, try to find out which types of touch she enjoys as well as those that irritate or offend her. I knew one husband who used to pat his wife on her butt until he discovered that it offended her so much that sexually she shut down completely.

Ask your wife to explain what "romance" means. Her answer may surprise you! But remember that whatever she says, she's giving you the tools to become a romantic all-day lover.

Make a list of a few of your favorite things about your wife. Share them with her.

Share your goals as a husband and father. Nothing will turn on your wife like loving your family.

Remember that your wife needs to hear the words "I love you"—and not just as you're walking out the door. She needs to hear those words throughout the day, in as many ways as you can express them verbally and nonverbally. To get you started in the right direction, we've listed a lot of ideas, but this list is by no means exhaustive. As you read through this list, think about what will work for you. Place a check by the ones that strike a chord with you and share them with your spouse.

1. *Let her sleep in.* Energy and sex drive are linked. A rested wife and mother makes for a rested lover, so at least one day this week, let her sleep in. Offer to take care of the kids and allow her to get some additional rest.

2. *Clean up after yourself in the bathroom.* Wash the whiskers down the sink. Use your towel to wipe off the sink. Then hang the towel up. The bathroom is an oasis for your wife.

3. *Make breakfast.* There's nothing like getting out of bed, getting ready and having no immediate chores to do. This adds to her rest.

4. *Keep the kids out.* Let her feet hit the bedroom floor and then the shower floor uninterrupted so that she can get ready free of distractions.

5. *Do a kid chore.* For example, offer to pick up the kids and say, "You go do something for you. I'll pick up the kids after school and take them with me."

6. *Bring her favorite morning beverage to her.* Waiting on your wife helps her feel pampered. Pampering helps her feel loved.

7. *Leave her notes around the house.* Post-it Notes are your best friends. When she opens the refrigerator door or a regularly used cabinet, make sure she sees a note that says something about how important she is to you: "I'm missing you." "You're the best!" "You're a great mom!" "How did I get blessed with you?"

8. *Put a load of laundry in or take out the trash before you leave for work.* Domestic support is tops on the list for getting her in the mood. This sort of action on your part gets the slow cooker to medium before 8:00 A.M. My personal goal right now is to take the trash out before my wife has to ask me. With a 13-gallon trash can, that means I'm usually taking the trash out two to three times a day.

9. *Give her one NST (Nonsexual Touch) before you leave for work.* Actually, if you can give her half a dozen of these a day, you are well on your way to passionate sexual intimacy. Embrace her before you leave for work and as soon as you get home. A pat or quick hug is not an embrace. Stop and take time to truly hug her.

10. *Call her from work.* Eighty percent of women fear disconnection. Anything you can do throughout the day that says, "I'm thinking about you," will prepare her. Call and let her know that you love her. Tell her how much you can't wait to see her. Find out the things she enjoys in order to prepare for your evening together.

11. *Email her.* You do not need to send her poetry or a five-page love letter, just a note to connect.

12. *Text her.* One affectionate line on her cell phone keeps you two connected, but don't overwhelm her.

13. *Send her vacation ads.* You may not be able to afford exotic vacations at this point in your life, but you can still dream and plan for them. Send your wife ads or pictures of travel destinations or vacations that you one day hope to take. Go with beaches, islands and tropical resorts rather than theme parks or sporting events.

14. *TiVo a movie.* Select a movie you know she has wanted to see and save a copy of it for her—or rent the DVD.

15. *Offer to bring home her favorite restaurant food.* This does not need to be fast food or anything fried. Larger sit-down restaurants are starting to take orders and designate special parking areas for those picking up carry-out.

16. *Bring home flowers and her favorite magazine.* She'll put the vase of flowers somewhere it can be seen often—and every time she sees it will be a reminder of you. She'll read the magazine while taking a bath after dinner—this is her time to relax and shave her legs.

17. *Eat a healthy meal.* Kelly Rippa, from the *Live with Regis and Kelly* show, once said that her husband knew when he was going to get sex: It was those nights when she ordered a salad instead of a burger.

18. *Hug and greet her before the kids.* Nothing shows your priority more than approaching her first. Hug your queen first, then reach for your prince or princess.

19. *Ask about her day first thing.* It does not need to be a 20-minute conversation. But before you start up the mower or take out the trash, get into a few details of her day.

20. *Give her time to exercise.* When a woman feels good about her body and health, she will feel better about sex. This is another idea that illustrates the link between energy and the sex drive.

21. *Clean up after dinner.* The sound of the dishwasher going is some of the best foreplay for Amy.

22. *Give the kids a bath.* Some of you are past this stage, but you can remember the exhaustion of those days. Nothing like ending your day trying to get an 18-month-old ready for bed. Relieve her of this task.

23. *Read books to the kids.* When I'm on the floor reading to my kids, Amy wants me. Funny how that works.

24. *Get rid of any distractions.* For young moms, that means hide the baby monitors and keep diapers off the nightstand. For all women, turn off the television. Television undermines healthy sexual relationships because couples end up watching just one last show. Without television, you'll end up sitting and talking and connecting emotionally and physically.

25. *Start the music.* From Andy Williams to a little Chicago—you know what music she likes. Take your iPod to work with you. If your wife is techno savvy, she'll know you took the time to download those songs at work. Va-va-voom!

26. *Apply lotions.* This one comes with a warning: Skip it if she has allergies, and remember that using too much lotion means you'll smell it for days.

27. *Light candles.* Candles are your next best friends after Post-it Notes. If your wife is insecure about her looks, use a votive in the far corner of the room.

28. *Give her a backrub.* A five-minute massage goes a long way to help your wife unwind.

29. *Offer a foot massage.* Nothing relaxes my wife more than relaxed feet.

30. *Rub her clitoris.* Ask her if this is permissible. Remember, guys, that she sets the boundaries in the bedroom.

31. *Be gentle.* Your wife wants a strong but gentle lover. By this time of the day, you have thought about sex a lot—you are raring to go. Don't put all your energy into the first 30 seconds. Treat sexual intimacy like a marathon, not a sprint.

Warning for Both the Husband and the Wife
*Above all, make sure all of your actions and words
of love for your mate are actually helping to
build your relationship. Dr. Gary Chapman
warns us that loving your mate the way you
like to be loved can actually communicate
that you're selfish and don't love your mate.*

The All-Day Female Lover

Tommy Nelson, pastor of Denton Bible Church in Denton, Texas, and conference speaker on the Song of Songs, says men are turned on by what they see and also by what they hear. While having intimate relations with their husband, most women have never heard the words, "Shhh! Be quiet!" Why? A husband likes to see his wife, he likes to hear her, and he likes to touch her and experience the fullness of who she is. Ladies, we have a list for you, too. Are you ready?

1. *Show up naked.* That's it. We don't need flowers, we don't need music, and most of us are fine even if the television is on.

2. *Pursue your man.* The greatest turn-on for a man is to be pursued by his wife. Knowing that Amy wants me physically is a huge turn-on for me. She pursues me and desires sexual intimacy with me. When a man initiates creativity, he often gets pigeonholed as perverse—or at least that is how I felt during the first half of our married life. When Amy initiates creativity, watch out! That's a recipe for great sex!

3. *Dress or undress slowly.* Get out of the closet. If you regularly tell your husband to turn away while you get your bra on, switch it up. Invite him to turn toward you as you get dressed. Or if you dress in the closet, invite him in for a minute or two to watch.

4. *Make noises.* Ladies, your husbands love it when you make noises. Nothing gets him more excited than knowing you are about to reach orgasm. He naturally wants to please you—but please, don't fake it.

5. *Change positions.* We are all prone to ruts in our sex life. If you are always the one on top, announce to your spouse that tonight you are on the bottom. If your spouse is always on top, announce that you will be on top tonight. Changing positions allows you to see, touch and feel your spouse in a new way.

6. *Change locations.* If you always have sex in the bedroom, consider experimenting in a different room of the house. Also, close the shades and add some natural excitement to your love life.

7. *Add a pillow.* Placing a pillow under the hips of the person on the bottom can change the angle and heighten the whole sexual experience. Try to find what works best for you.

8. *Burn the sweats.* If you and your husband go to bed every night dressed head to toe, go to bed naked one night with no intention of having sex.

9. *Take a shower.* You may be thinking, *We shower in the morning.* But getting clean is not the goal of this shower. Turn on the water and be very careful.

10. *Buy satin sheets or sheets with a higher thread count.* Amy taught me this valuable lesson. One day while shopping in Target—her favorite store—she suddenly became extremely excited when she saw 500 thread-count sheets on the clearance rack. It was as if Dewalt or Craftsman tools were on sale. I had no idea a woman could get so excited over linens. But when we slipped into bed that night, I finally understood her excitement. Nice! We have not splurged for satin yet, but that day is definitely coming soon.

11. *Decorate the room as an exotic vacation destination.* We decorate for birthday parties, so why not for a night of passion and romance? Decorate the room as a Hawaiian or a mountain resort. Tear out pictures from magazines. Place some fine chocolate on the pillows. Put appropriate flowers on the nightstand. Find other small ways to change the atmosphere.

12. *Get out of the house.* I (Gary) have a good friend who told me that one night while he and his wife were driving through the city, shopping for a car (they were looking to trade in their family van), the urge hit them—and they ended up pulling their van into a parking lot and going at it like it was their first time. Talk about spontaneous! He was laugh-

ing when he told me this story, and he said he and his wife still laugh about it months later. Another idea is one I accidentally overheard my adult children discussing: They were telling each other what department-store dressing room they most liked having sex in.

13. *Explore the great outdoors.* Another friend of mine shared that he and his wife take turns each month planning a special intimate night together (they have sex more than one time a month, but these are special nights). Last month was my friend's turn, so he created a private "bedroom" in their backyard, under the stars. They had sex on the trampoline. Baby lotion was the key ingredient. (The manufacturers of the trampoline did not put a warning label on the equipment, so let this serve as your warning.)

14. *Be predictably unpredictable.* If you eventually settle on three or maybe four of the above-mentioned creative elements in your sex life, keep switching them. If your spouse never knows which one is coming, spice and anticipation will be added to the mix.

15. *Enjoy a quickie.* For Meryl and Anthony, the only way they could pull off a Sunday-afternoon quickie was to send their eight-year-old son out on the balcony with a Popsicle and tell him to report on all the neighborhood activities.

While in bed, the couple could hear their son announcing, "There's a car being towed down the street."

A few moments later he shouted, "An ambulance just drove by."

"Looks like the Anderson's have company," he called out.

"Matt's riding a new bike!" he declared with a trace of envy.

"Looks like the Sanders are moving," he proclaimed.

"Jason is on his skateboard," he yelled.

Benefits of a Quickie

- Provides release
- Lowers risk of sexual temptation
- Validates husband's wiring
- Allows for prolonged sex later in the week

Cautions of a Quickie

- Can invalidate a wife's desire for orgasm
- Too many are exhausting for the typical wife

"The Coopers are having sex!" he announced confidently.

Startled, Meryl and Anthony jumped out of bed. Anthony called out, "Son, how do you know they're having sex?"

"Because Jimmy Cooper is standing on his balcony with a Popsicle, too."

Let's face it: The quickie isn't easy—especially if you have children. But a quickie can go a long way to spicing up your sex life. One of the best tips I ever heard on quickies is something Steve Doocy taught me in his book *The Mr. and Mrs. Happy Handbook: Everything I Know About Love and Marriage (with Corrections by Mrs. Doocy)*: If you want to pull off a quickie in the middle of the afternoon with preschoolers, place two sets of shoes in the dryer and set it for 30 minutes. Two important things happen: (1) You have a timer—most men won't need a half hour, but it's there just in case; (2) The dryer becomes the loudest activity in the house.

Flavoring Your Sexual Experience

Food plays an important role in sex and sexual situations.[1] After all, physical energy is one of the keys to great sex. Experts say that when you're well fed and healthy, you're more interested in sexual activities. That means that a healthy and nutritious diet is of great benefit to a satisfactory sexual life—spicing it up and energizing it.

Nutritious foods provide the energy you need for sexual activity. And if you're a healthy eater, you'll be more passionate during sex. Good food also increases creativity, and creativity will always enhance your love life.

The following foods are believed to help lift your mood:

· Almond	· Carrot	· Milk	· Soybean
· Apple	· Chicken	· Peanut	· Spinach
· Beet	· Egg	· Pineapple	· Tomato

The following foods are considered sensual foods:

· Whipped Cream · Chocolate   · Strawberries   · Grapes

With the right romantic attitude, any meal can be turned into a memorable sexual experience. Start by taking the initiative to prepare the dinner, or help your spouse prepare the food. When dinner is ready, suggest that before you enjoy the meal together, both of you should slip into something seductive. Feed each other creatively—body parts can become plates and napkins, and your tongue can help you get the most of every bite. Enjoy every moment of eating together. By the end of the meal, you may end up making love on the dining table—who knows?

Letting Your Fingers Do the Walking

I (Ted) have a very weak stomach. At the sight of blood, I pass out. On a recent hospital visit, the doctor came in and began describing the situation; next thing I knew, I was on a hospital gurney, sipping a Kool-Aid drink. Anatomical exploration can make me woozy! I get light-headed, my palms sweat, and my knees weaken. And all I can do is look for a place to sit and put my head between my knees.

Now the reason I described my weak stomach is because in doing research for this book, late one night (so now you must add the fact that I was tired) I was reading *Sheet Music: Uncovering the Secrets of Sexual Intimacy in Marriage,* a book my friend Dr. Kevin Leman wrote. I was reading at the dining-room table. When I read the following section on finding your wife's G-spot, my wooziness kicked in:

First off, men, let me caution you—the G-spot is not a trigger that can be pushed to set off fireworks at will. You've got to work your way toward it. If you jam some fingers up there and start fishing around, you're liable to turn your wife into a killer whale rather than a purring kitten. Do your work first, and once your wife is already aroused, gently insert one or two fingers (your palm should be facing you) into her vagina. This next part varies from woman to woman, but in general, about one or two inches above the vagina's opening, on the front wall, you'll eventually feel a small spot that has a few ridges, or that feels a little rougher than the surrounding skin. Since you are touching the urethra, your wife may worry that she needs to urinate—but soon, if you keep applying gentle pressure, that urge will collapse into a very pleasant sensation. You'll know you hit the jackpot when the moans soon follow.[2]

Whoa! I'll have to admit the vivid and detailed approach of Dr. Leman made all the blood rush to my head—some things are better done than talked about.

Some guys may be timid about penetrating their wife with their fingers. They approach this with great caution. Keep this in mind: During sex, the penis is thrusting inside the vagina to a much stronger degree. It also goes much deeper than a finger can reach. Talk it through with your wife. If she is not comfortable with you searching for her G-spot, then this is off-limits. If she permits the exploration, proceed with gentleness and passion.

A Caution for Couples Exhausted or Intimidated After Reading This Chapter

If this chapter has exhausted or intimidated you, don't stress. Some of the best sex is the simplest. Creativity is not meant to exhaust or frustrate you. You may end up only getting creative once a month or every other month, and that is okay. There are no rules here for spicing it up.

Also, you both must be good with these spices. If your spouse is uncomfortable with something, do not do it. Do not push it. Remember that sex is not meant to ever be used as a weapon or a reward.

I only eat red velvet cake on special occasions, mainly birthdays. It is not a cake typically available at restaurants. When I walk into a party and see red velvet cake with cream-cheese frosting, my eyes light up and I start justifying a generous portion. Creative sex works much the same way. Let it be spontaneous and periodic. Keep each other guessing.

In the next chapter, we will show you the links between your sexuality and your spirituality. The depth of one affects the other. If you have struggles with sexual intimacy, the next chapter will encourage you to start by pursuing intimacy with God.

From GarySmalley.com

Q: My wife and I have a great marriage. We have created security in our marriage, yet the bedroom still has problems. Physical intimacy is very difficult for my wife. How can I help?

A: Understand her. Without trying to change or manipulate her, discover ways to comfort her in what she is feeling when it comes to sex.

Dr. Catherine Hart Weber has helped many couples in the area of sexual healing. Here's a key factor affecting many marriages today:

Sexuality—who you are deep within yourself—not just genital things or sexual things but who you are as a person at the deepest possible level. Sex is dangerous outside of God's design. When contained within God's design it brings wholeness and healing, but outside of it, it brings destruction and misery. Sex has implications that go way beyond the moment of joy. The greatest potential for sin lies in the area of our sexuality. When we use people for sex, we deface the beauty of the sexual experience. The casualties are mainly women and children.

In a recent study, we asked women what their history was—what had their past sexual experiences been like? A lot of women talked about experiencing some kind of sexual trauma—something in their history that hadn't been according to God's design. Women talked about unplanned pregnancies, abortions, giving children up for adoption, STDs, sexual abuse. Interestingly, most of the women had experienced being touched in a way they didn't want by a relative or somebody who was a caregiver. Emotional trauma—women talked about having flashbacks. Conflict in their current marriage—things they felt were blocked in their marriage because of past sexual experiences.[3]

Sexual trauma deeply affects the physical intimacy between a husband and wife. There are many factors that can affect a women's desire for sex, including but not limited to her menstrual cycle, depression or lack of energy from her job or the kids.

How can you help? Learn how to ask great questions. Let your questions have the goal of healing and not just sex. Let your wife know that her wholeness—spiritually, physically and emotionally—is your goal. Your questions will lead to greater understanding. And understanding will only create greater security in your marriage.

Work to get into your wife's heart. This is the deepest level of communication you can have. The goal of level 6 communication in this case is not to get sex but rather to know your wife at a greater level of understanding. When she feels safe, she may begin to open up about what is really going on.

As you ask great questions of your wife, ask great questions of yourself as well. Can you observe any activities in the home that are depleting your wife's energy at night? Is there anything you can do to help her reserve energy, like clean up after dinner or picking up around the house? What other ways can you serve or work to create security and meet her desires?

The heart of sex is security. Look and pray for ways each day to build that into your marriage. This will help you develop the spiritual dimension of your sex life.

Notes
1. This section is based on "Role of Diet in Sex," *Levitra Bliss*, 2006. http://www.levitrabliss.com/role_diet_in_sex.html (accessed August 2007).
2. Kevin Leman, *Sheet Music: Uncovering the Secrets of Sexual Intimacy in Marriage* (Carol Stream, IL: Tyndale House Publishers, 2003), p. 129.
3. Catherine Hart Weber, "Redeeming Sexuality in Marriage" (lecture, Saddleback Community Church, Orange County, CA, October 4, 1998).

Summary

Creativity in your marriage takes a lot of work, but the payoff is huge.

"Creativity" and "sex" in the same sentence are *not* perverted or dirty words.

Creativity is healthy and can be enjoyed guilt-free and with greater passion than ever.

The work it takes to be creative and unpredictable is not always possible. Kids, work schedules and household chores can crowd out creativity. A solution is the quickie. (*Caution:* Like fast food, a steady diet of quickies is not healthy.)

Pillow Talk

A few of my favorite things about you are . . .

My goals as a husband and a father are . . .

How do you feel about introducing quickies into our marriage for the days when life is crazy and it has been awhile since we've been intimate?

What concerns do you have about quickies?

What can we do to bring our sex life out of a "rut"?

CHAPTER 10

The Spiritual Dimensions of Sex

Sex is so much more than just a physical act. Sex is an emotional and spiritual experience. Gina Ogden, a sex therapist researching at Harvard University, is the author of the book *Women Who Love Sex*. She is currently studying the connection between women, sex and spirituality. She says, "The key to deeper satisfaction is connecting sexuality to spirituality."[1] In other words, sexuality and spirituality go together. The most sexually fulfilled women were also the most spiritual women. When you miss the spiritual dimension that's naturally a part of sex, you miss out on part of the pleasure.

Whether you realize it or not, your spiritual life affects your sex life. A healthy spiritual life affects your relationship, your attitude and your emotions. That's one reason why it's so important to maintain a spiritual connection in your marriage.

Countless couples have shared with us how their relationship is strengthened and enriched when they pray together. Couples who attend church together, worship together and attend Bible studies together discover things about each other that they would never learn otherwise.

Marriage researchers Scott Stanley and Howard Markman conducted a nationwide phone survey to determine where the best sex is found. Their research showed that married people have sex more often and enjoy sex more than singles. Couples living together but not married have more sex than married couples, but nothing is said about the quality.[2]

Why do married couples enjoy sex more? One word: *commitment*. And spiritual commitment deepens great sex all the more.

One of the reasons faith in God is so important is that without the context of a faith-based value system, information can be misused to manipulate people. Knowledge in the context of faith brings value, meaning and an expression that you otherwise don't get. In this chapter, we'll explore the spiritual dimensions of sex and introduce you to four spiritual commitments that will transform your relationship with God and your spouse.

The Four Spiritual Commitments

Four spiritual commitments you can make to your mate today can change your marriage and sexual intimacy forever.

1. I Will Remove the Expectation that My Mate Will Meet All My Needs
Pledging not to expect your spouse to meet all of your needs is a simple but powerful commitment that takes the pressure off your spouse. God never created Adam or Eve as a replacement for Himself. Throughout the story of creation, we read that God looked at the light, the water, the vegetation and the animals, and they were all good. But when it came to the creation of man, God said it wasn't good—man needed a suitable helper. Nothing in creation was an appropriate companion or counterpart to him. So God made the first woman.

But since the Fall and the eviction from the Garden, many men and women have tried to replace their relationship with God with their relationship with each other. We expect our spouse to become one of our main sources of life and joy. The result is codependence.

Codependence is created when we rely on people, places or things to make or keep us happy. Codependents cope by blaming the other person for their unhappiness. We all have a tendency toward codependence. It sounds like this:

"If you would stop doing that, then I would stop."
"You started this argument."

"I said I do because I assumed you would."

"We have money problems that are destroying our marriage."

"You are making me mad."

"If my husband would change a few of his annoying habits, we would have a much better marriage."

"If my wife would quit nagging, I'd do a lot better."

"It's my boss's fault for my poor attitude at night."

Philippians 4:19 says, "My God will meet all your needs according to his glorious riches in Christ Jesus." Within the context of the verse, Paul is encouraging the Church, but the principle extends into all of our lives. God is ultimately the One who meets our needs. He is the source of all that we are and will be.

Whenever we begin to look to our spouse to meet all of our needs, we will be disappointed and feel let down. Eventually this will grow into a feeling of being unappreciated and even resentful. There are times in all of our relationships when we will feel like we're getting the short end of the stick.

Even in my (Ted's) own marriage, I sometimes wonder if anyone appreciates me. Just recently, I was sweating heavily in 100-degree heat, mowing the lawn up a 12-degree incline. I didn't have the best attitude. Was I mowing the lawn for the praise of my wife and appreciation of the whole family? Or was I mowing the lawn because it is the right and responsible thing to do? What did I want? Selfish Ted wanted applause. *I'm not asking for a marching band, but some appreciation would be nice.* That attitude reeks of codependence.

> *Whenever we begin to look to our spouse*
> *to meet all of our needs, we will be*
> *disappointed and feel let down.*

Whenever your behavior is motivated by the action or reaction of your mate, you are setting yourself up for failure. You are to do the right thing no matter how your spouse responds or reacts. You are 100-percent responsible for you.

So the challenge in all of our marriages is simply this: Let your mate off the hook. Don't expect your mate to meet all of your needs. Make a commitment to do everything you can to drop your expectations.

Your mate was never created to form your deepest love, honor or security. It's God's job to be our highest and best Friend and our loving King. All of the laws of Scripture can be boiled down to just two commandments: Love God and love others. It's a lot more hopeful and relaxing to know clearly what God's will is and that He will even give you the power to live it. He is love, and He gives love freely to those who crave to know and serve Him. I try to start every day with the truth that God loves me more than anyone else does or can, and He desires to give me more and more of His power and love. I truly want to know Him better today than I did yesterday. And I love hiding His powerful, living words within my heart in order to not only know Him better but also to do His will better.

2. I Will Make Every Effort to Seek My Fulfillment from God

Dr. Bob Paul of the National Institute of Marriage said something intriguing: "There are so many things out there that will be attractive to an unfulfilled person." In other words, unfulfillment is the fuel of addiction.

We fall into this trap of unfulfillment whenever we begin thinking that if we just had a little more of _____ (fill in the blank), life would be complete. Maybe it's more money, time or toys. You may think more children, the right job or just a few more weeks of vacation would make all the difference in your life. But as we said, the truth is that real fulfillment comes from a vibrant relationship with God. That means pursuing God no matter what the circumstances, no matter how bad it gets.

I (Ted) first became involved in ministry at the age of 22. I was serving at a church in Georgia and eagerly asked the head pastor, "The next time the funeral home calls and asks you to do a funeral and you're unable to do it, would you recommend me?" Shortly afterward, the pastor received a call from a funeral home. The person who died didn't have a home church or family in the area.

Because it was my first funeral, I wore my best suit. I was scared and thrilled all at the same time. I was surprised to discover that this particular funeral parlor had a mourning room, which meant the family would sit behind a dark curtain veil during the service. I was standing beside the open casket when I began to hear an 8-track play "Amazing Grace." At the end of the song, the funeral director gave me a nod.

I wasn't quite sure what the nod meant. Besides two family members behind the curtain, the funeral director and the deceased, no one else came. I walked toward the director and quietly asked, "Where are all the people?"

"This guy wasn't very liked," he whispered.

I walked back up to the front and began to preach. I remember looking at the curtain standing between myself and the family members and thinking, *This is one of the most insane things I'd ever done in my life.* But I had passion and energy, and I preached one of the best messages I've ever given.

Too often, marriages resemble that funeral experience. A veil of disconnect separates the husband and wife. Your mate is there, but you don't really see him or you don't really hear her. One person may be passionate and full of energy for God, but the other is withdrawn or unmoved.

When you make every effort to seek your fulfillment from God, you'll find yourself not just lavished in God's love but also better able to lavish your spouse with love.

First Peter 3 is an encouraging passage for those in that situation. It describes a believing wife married to an unbelieving husband and says that the husband will take notice of the change in her life. In other words, when you pursue the Lord with all your heart, soul, mind and strength, you can't help but be transformed. When you are truly growing in the Lord, you will naturally become a more gentle, kind and loving person. That means that you don't wait for your spouse to go to church, start reading the Bible, join a small group or pray every day. Instead, you live your life as an example of those things and more. When you make every effort to seek your fulfillment from God, you'll find yourself not just lavished in God's love but also better able to lavish your spouse with love.

The real secret to creating more hunger in your spouse if he or she does not believe in God is by letting your mate see a model of someone becoming more like God without any signs of criticism from you about his or her behavior. Most people haven't seen a person who has hidden God's words within his or her heart and thus been led to godly transformation, or who has submitted to the Holy Spirit and thus has received amazing power to both love and bless others. When these two habits are formed in you, your unbelieving mate can discover the reality of God and His ways. When you're not being critical, your spouse gets to witness a real live model of God's transforming power in action.

3. I Will Take 100-Percent Responsibility for My Spiritual Journey
When I perform marriage ceremonies and a couple wants to use a unity candle as a part of the service, I no longer have the couple blow out the two candles once they light the middle one. Instead, I have them keep their individual candles lit. I understand the imagery behind oneness as part of the tradition. However, taken to the extreme, this leads to codependence. There are three journeys: your journey, your mate's journey and the marital journey. Three lit candles best represent the truth that a marriage relationship is between the husband, the wife and God.

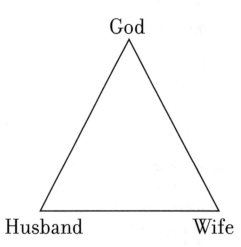

168

As we pursue God together, the distance between us grows smaller. If you are a follower of Jesus Christ, if you have been converted and have confessed Him as Lord and boss of your life, and if you believe that He has been raised from the dead and you are a saved person who is now growing in the faith—you have the spirit of God living within you. He is not in this building. He is not in a temple or in a structure or in an idol built by human hands. The Bible says *you* are now the temple of the living God.

Ephesians 3:16-18 says, "I pray that out of his glorious riches he may strengthen you with power through his Spirit in your inner being, so that Christ may dwell in your hearts through faith. And I pray that you, being rooted and established in love, may have power, together with all the saints, to grasp how wide and long and high and deep is the love of Christ."

In other words, the deeper you grow in your relationship with Christ, the more loving you will be.

What did Jesus say? He didn't say we are known as His disciples by the way we get even, the way we nag, the way we always have to be right. He said we are known as His disciples by the way we love each other.

Jesus has called us to love, even when the person is unlovable. The reward is amazing!

> Since, then, you have been raised with Christ, set your hearts on things above, where Christ is seated at the right hand of God. Set your minds on things above, not on earthly things. For you died, and your life is now hidden with Christ in God. When Christ, who is your life, appears, then you also will appear with him in glory.
>
> Put to death, therefore, whatever belongs to your earthly nature: sexual immorality, impurity, lust, evil desires and greed, which is idolatry. Because of these, the wrath of God is coming. You used to walk in these ways, in the life you once lived. But now you must rid yourselves of all such things as these: anger, rage, malice, slander, and filthy language from your lips. Do not lie to each other, since you have taken off your old self with

its practices and have put on the new self, which is being renewed in knowledge in the image of its Creator. . . .

Let the peace of Christ rule in your hearts, since as members of one body you were called to peace. And be thankful. Let the word of Christ dwell in you richly as you teach and admonish one another with all wisdom, and as you sing psalms, hymns and spiritual songs with gratitude in your hearts to God. And whatever you do, whether in word or deed, do it all *in the name of the Lord Jesus, giving thanks to God the Father through him* (Col. 3:1-17, emphasis added).

This passage gives you unlimited power. You are not held hostage to a bad marriage or a derelict spouse. You do not have to stay in the pit. You can get up every day and take responsibility for the way you will embrace the day. You can have peace in your heart by focusing on Christ and eternity. Your husband or wife is not in charge of your mind or heart.

As a pastor, I spend my days urging people to crawl out of the muck and mire. It is a depressing place to live, but most of the time I have to fight with people to get them out. As humans, we can get very comfortable in misery. And that includes our marriages. For example, meet Fred and Cheryl.

I met Fred and Cheryl while they were separated. After 15 years of marriage, Cheryl was done playing the games. I have counseled many couples out of extramarital affairs, but I had never seen anything like the pit this couple lived in. These two used affairs to get even with each other. By the time they got to me, Fred had been with eight different women in those 15 years and Cheryl had been with six different men. It was retaliatory sex. This was the first couple I had ever met who truly hated each other. It was also the first time I used Jesus' "love your enemies" command in marriage counseling (see Matt. 5:44; Luke 6:27,35).

Fred and Cheryl's home was toxic. Remember in chapter 5 when we talked about the levels of communication? We said that Levels 1 (small talk) and 2 (facts) have little to no risk of escalated argument. Fred and

Cheryl, however, were cursing each other at Level 1: "Could I have the @&*#ing salt?" "What the @#$% for?"

Where do you start with a couple this angry? I started with an observation: "Fred. Cheryl. It's obvious that you two hate each other. And it's apparent that you don't have a marriage here. I rarely, if ever, counsel divorce, but in this case I must in order to prevent a murder—but I need to ask you a question. Do I have your permission to ask you a spiritual question?"

"I guess," Fred mumbled.

"What if I told you both that you do not have a marital problem?" I asked.

"Huh?" Cheryl asked surprisingly.

"You do not have a problem with sex or even a problem with salt." I continued, "What's going on in your marriage, and in your bed, and with the saltshakers at dinner, well, those are just symptoms of a greater need."

"Jesus, right?" Fred asked reluctantly. After all, they were in a pastor's office.

"Fred, all of your anger, rage and discontentment stem from the lack of fulfillment in your life," I said. "You must resolve your anger with the only true source of life."

Fred, Cheryl and I met more than a dozen more times after that first session. That was just the beginning of their new life in Christ. I encouraged them with a key to understanding spiritual growth: Take responsibility for your own—and only your own—spiritual journey. You must identify your own need for Christ to fill the emptiness in your life. This first step begins a journey, not a race. Too often we like to package life change in a nice and neat 6- or 13-week Bible study. This has created a faulty idea that life change happens fast. I believe real life change is typically slow. I like to think in terms of years, not weeks or months. This alone should encourage a couple not to think their marriage will be perfect or on track after a few sessions with a pastor or counselor. Give it time. Fred and Cheryl spent more than a dozen weeks just taking the first step: taking 100-percent personal responsibility for their separate spiritual journeys. That is where their joint journey of healing began.

4. I Will Make God, Not My Mate, the Center of My Life

Imagine a blue plastic bucket for a moment. Now imagine the bucket has a supply of clean, crystal-clear water from God. It never runs out. But unlike the bucket, your mate has limitations. Unlike the bucket, your mate will eventually run out. Your mate isn't going to have the energy to meet every one of your needs. Jesus told the lady who was coming with her bucket to get water from the well that she was going to get thirsty again. But Jesus promised that if she drank from Him, she would not thirst again.

When you commit yourself to a vibrant relationship with God, you become like that blue bucket. You find yourself filled and refilled by God Himself day after day. You find yourself renewed and ready to be poured out to your spouse, your family and your community.

Before I (Gary) get out of bed each morning, I like to quote Colossians 3:15—"Let the peace of Christ rule in your hearts"—as a prayer. Why do I do that? Colossians 3:16 advises, "Let the word of Christ dwell in you richly as you teach and admonish one another with all wisdom, and as you sing psalms, hymns and spiritual songs with gratitude in your hearts to God." When we practice simple spiritual disciplines like prayer, worship and fellowship, we get filled up, and the peace of Christ rules in our hearts. When our focus is on God, then our spouses naturally get to enjoy the overflow.

Too often, couples believe that their happiness is based on each other. But our real happiness, our true joy, is based on our individual relationship with God. Couples often say they need help with their marriage, as if they don't have problems as individuals—it's just when they get together that their problems and sin manifest themselves. They blame their marriage for the issues—but the issues were in place before the marriage.

There are a variety of unhealthy questions people ask as they get married, including:

- What's in it for me?
- Will I be happy?
- Is this person going to care for me?
- Is this person going to provide for me?

- Is this person going to meet all of my needs?
- Is this person my soul mate?

Some people believe their marriage is bad because they didn't marry their soul mate. That's simply not true. The concept of soul mates (sometimes referred to as twin souls) has its roots in the idea of reincarnation. The soul of the one you are looking for has lived other lives with your past selves, and your souls have connected. Plato, an ancient Greek philosopher, referred to a soul mate as the other half. The concept of a soul mate has no biblical basis and sets up an excusable escape for couples.

Too often, couples believe that their happiness is based on each other. But our real happiness, our true joy, is based on our individual relationships with God.

I've had married people tell me, "Well, I think he is a great guy—he's just not the guy for me," and "I think she's wonderful and she'll make somebody very happy—she's just not making me happy." These are the wrong perspectives for sustaining a healthy marriage.

What are the right questions? Here is the foundation for getting your marriage off on the right foot and staying there:

- Am I demonstrating the loving image and character of Jesus Christ? If I'm not, I need to get His words into my heart so that I don't sin against God or my mate.

- Have I taken responsibility for my own actions and reactions? If not, I need to get off of my mate's case and get the help I need from God first and then from other wise counsel.

- Do I understand that within me there is a self-destructive sin nature that only God can fix?

- Do I understand that I make mistakes, I fail and I grieve the heart of God?

- Have I ever cried out to God as a beggar and admitted that I am helpless apart from Him in becoming the mate I need to be?

- Do I understand that because of Adam and Eve, I am now dealing with inherited sin?

- Do I know that sin is basically doing my own thing and ignoring God?

- When my spouse sees my deep love and transformation, will he or she want to join me on the spiritual journey?

The Bible says that "all have sinned and fall short of the glory of God" (Rom. 3:23). We all deal with this issue of sin. The question is how do we respond? Romans 10:9-10 instructs us to declare Him as Lord (or as boss) of our life and believe in our heart that God has raised Jesus from the dead; then, the Bible says, we will be saved. It is a one-time decision (justification) followed by or made evident in lifestyle change (sanctification).

When I (Ted) ask couples to share their spiritual journey, I am generally taken back to a time when they prayed a prayer, walked down an aisle or stood up during a prayer at camp. I celebrate those decisions, but I also look for the fruit. I want to know about their spiritual journey, not just their conversion time and date. Too many couples treat their conversions as good enough and do not work to know God more. Because life change happens from the inside out, that is where marriage change begins as well. I am not concerned with a couple's parents' faith or the church they grew up in. I am interested in what they are doing today to know God.

I don't know of anything more powerful than to memorize 10 dynamite Bible verses and chew on them every day for the remainder of your life. You'll begin to see amazing changes and more love for each other than you ever imagined. Remember that God's Word is alive, powerful and sharper than a two-edged sword (see Heb. 4:12).

Here is what I love about growing like Christ: We begin to experience what we already are by God's grace. We are declared righteous. Becoming like Christ is not earning salvation; it is being conformed to His image, which is what He has called us to be. Most couples in crisis haven't come to this place. They struggle because their sinful natures have gotten the best of them and one or both spouses have become codependent. They expect their mates to meet their needs and make them happy.

The true mark of maturity, though, is the ability to experience the joy-filled Christian life no matter what the circumstances.

This same principle applies to the workplace. Your boss isn't making you miserable. He or she may be difficult to work with, but Paul said we are to do our work as unto the Lord (see Col. 3:23). My marriage is to be a place, an institution, where I am to love Amy as unto the Lord. She is to love me as unto the Lord.

The Bible says we are to submit to one another out of reverence for Christ, out of what Christ has done. How then do we show gratefulness and thankfulness? Out of reverence for Christ, love your spouse—even when your spouse is unlovable. It's a mark of maturity. Remember that people, places and things will never fill you up to overflowing. They are not the source of having your needs met. God, not your mate, is the only One who can meet all your needs.

Connecting Spiritually with Your Lover

Fire Your Mate!
Tell your wife or husband that she or he is no longer in charge of your moods, emotions, words or reactions. You will no longer blame your spouse for your shortcomings or hold him or her accountable for your spiritual journey.

Accept the Job!
Take responsibility. Step up to the plate and begin your journey of faith and feed it for yourself first.

Recruit Assistants!

You are the CEO of your life, but you can ask your mate for assistance or help. How can he or she help? Here are several ways to assist one another:

- Pray for each other daily.
- Pray with each other daily.
- Read a book together but at different times and places from each other. Use dinners or dates to discuss what you are learning.
- Draft a spiritual constitution or a family contract stating the four commitments from this chapter. Sign it together. Maybe even have a judge or pastor sign it with you. As your kids grow older, they can sign their own with you.

The best sex of your life has a rich spiritual dimension. In the next chapter, we're going to help you discover how to resolve conflict in your marriage—before it begins.

From GarySmalley.com

Q: How do you deal with a husband who is slowly getting cold toward the things of God and becoming addicted to pornography?

A: Let me validate you for a moment. Catching your husband viewing porn invokes feelings similar to mourning a death. My wife has told me that if she ever caught me viewing porn, it would be no different than walking into the bedroom and catching me with another woman. It hurts and destroys all trust in the relationship. Women in no way, shape or form want to have their looks and body compared to that of another woman. But when a husband views porn, that is exactly what he is doing. He is saying, "My wife no longer is enough. I must go outside of the marriage to be stimulated."

Viewing porn is an addictive behavior that needs treatment similar to the detoxification that an alcoholic or drug addict goes through.

The pain is deep. I am not asking you to put a mask over your pain and act as though it did not happen. You must guard your heart from bitterness. You and your husband are equally valuable to God.

God is the only One who can change a human heart. In your husband's case, it sounds like he is filling his need for a relationship with God and others with an addiction.

I encourage you to etch the words of 1 Peter 3 on your heart. It is a very encouraging passage, and it is full of insight for a believing wife on how to influence her unbelieving husband. It says, "Your godly lives will speak to them better than any words. They will be won over by watching your pure, godly behavior" (1 Pet. 3:1-2, *NLT*). The key to remember: You can't change him.

Avoid preaching at him. You've probably already learned that it doesn't work. Pray for him every day. Watch the way you live in front of him. If he sees you always on him for his addiction and in turn he sees you gossiping on the phone to your friends or lying to a boss or friend, he may use that hypocrisy as an excuse to not grow in his own walk with the Lord. Watch your own behavior and be very careful to not come across as though you are free from sin.

Let him know that you love him, and be vulnerable with your own struggles in life and the pain that this has caused you. Honesty and vulnerability are both within the spirit of 1 Peter 3. Above all else, hold out hope that God can still change him, yet put the focus on God changing you. Watch what happens when your husband sees you growing and becoming more like Christ every day.

Notes

1. "Sex and Spirituality," Oprah.com. http://www.oprah.com/relationships/relationships_con tent.jhtml?contentId=con_20020916_sexspirit.xml&section=Sex&subsection=Sex (accessed October 2007).
2. Scott M. Stanley and Howard J. Markman, *Marriage in the 90s: A Nationwide Random Phone Survey*, PREP, Inc., May 26, 1997. http://www.prepinc.com/main/docs/marriage_90s_1997.pdf (accessed August 2007).

Summary

Sex is so much more than just a physical act—
it is an emotional and spiritual experience.

Your spiritual life affects your sex life.

Remove the expectation that your mate will meet
all your needs. Make every effort to seek your
fulfillment from God.

Take 100-percent responsibility for your
own spiritual journey.

Make God, not your mate, the center of your life.

Too often, couples believe that happiness is based
on each other. Real happiness—true joy—is based
on our individual relationships with God.

Pillow Talk

Do you think that I demonstrate the loving image
and character of Jesus Christ?

Do you believe that I take responsibility for my
own actions and reactions?

What are some ways we can bring our spiritual
lives more deeply into our relationship?

CHAPTER 11

Resolve Conflict

While there aren't any scientific studies that I (Ted) know of that tell us what percentage of couples fight on their honeymoon, I bet the statistics would surprise us—or maybe not! Like most couples, Amy and I fought on our honeymoon. We were in the Bahamas on a four-day cruise. She told me ahead of time that she wanted to go snorkeling, and I responded, "I'd love to go snorkeling with you!" Little did I know!

We got on one of those fiesta barges with about 150 other people. The boat was packed full of people and equipment. Looking at the pile of snorkels, I couldn't help but wonder, *How many people have put their mouths on those?* Ew! Once I selected a snorkel, I slipped a bottle of antibacterial gel out of my pocket and began rubbing it on the mouth of the snorkel. Amy looked at me as if I was from a different planet but didn't say a word.

We had to stand in a long line to get into the water, and in a desire to speed things up I went ahead and began putting on my mask, snorkel and fins. We were still toward the end of the line when I was ready to jump in. Now I know I looked like a total nerd, but I figured, *Hey, I'm married now, so who cares?* Not wanting to miss a minute in the water, I suggested to my new bride that she begin getting ready. She responded, "I think I'm going to wait until we're at the water's edge. That way I can put my feet in the water and let them acclimate to the temperature. I'll get my knees wet and then I'll put my equipment on."

While her logic was impeccable, I was far more concerned with slowing down the line (even though we were toward the end of it). As we neared the front of the line, I encouraged her again, "We're almost there—put your mask and fins on!"

"No," she pushed back. "I'm getting in slowly."

"But there are all these people behind us," I exclaimed. "And this is embarrassing."

"They're fine," she said confidently.

Now Amy is never worried about what other people think—it's very much a gift that God has given her—and it makes her a great pastor's wife. But on that fateful day, I didn't appreciate her gift. In fact, I was mad. When it was our turn to get into the water, I committed a classic honeymoon blunder: I pushed her in.

To make matters worse, I jumped in and shouted, "Come on, Amy! Let's go!" Not only did she lose one of her fins, but she also lost respect for me. I was an immature jerk and didn't even realize it. My new wife hated every minute of our time in the water and when we finally got on board the boat, I realized just how bad I had messed up. She was so ticked off at me that even by dinner, things hadn't cooled down. That fight robbed me of almost two days of our honeymoon!

We will all experience moments of anger and conflict with our spouses. That's natural. But the difference between a good relationship and a great one is how you respond to the conflicts. And nowhere is that more apparent than when conflict plays out in our sex lives. This tension is nothing new—it's something that even Solomon experienced. In this chapter, we're going to uncover four intruders that cause conflict in your relationship. Then we're going to teach you how to handle conflict in the most intimate of places—the bedroom. Finally, we're going to give you the best possible anecdote to conflict.

Intruders of Intimacy

Sometimes little things can creep into our marriages that impede intimacy. Solomon calls these *foxes*: "Catch for us the foxes, the little foxes that ruin the vineyards, our vineyards that are in bloom" (Song of Songs 2:15). In those days foxes were the most destructive animals to the vineyards. They could destroy an entire vineyard by eating the buds before they bloomed. If they ate enough buds, they could wipe out an entire crop.

Our modern vineyard is our marriage, and the foxes represent anything that can undermine growth and fruitfulness. We want to introduce you to four of these intruders, because you will face them at some point in your marriage.

1. Escalation

Escalation sneaks in when we start defending or trying to win an argument. This intruder invites you to volley back and forth with accusatory and defensive statements. You invite this intruder into your marriage whenever you say, "It's your fault," "You always . . ." or "You never . . ."

Escalation is an intruder that sneaks in quietly but quickly. Many times, escalation shows up because we have bottled up our feelings and emotions. In a single moment, something happens and *snap!*—we let it all out. Escalation works much like a volcano. You never know when it is going to erupt, and you usually cannot control the flow.

The main reason why escalation and the other three intruders disconnect us from our mate and harm our marriage is because all four usually leave both mates with *unresolved anger*. Unresolved anger kills love. Anger not only darkens our hearts, but when we are angry and stay mad, anger also seems to push love out of our heart. We can't know the light of God or His love, and we walk around the house as a blind person, unable to see our way back into harmony.

2. Harsh Language

Notice we did not say curse words or foul language. That alone would not cover it. The Bible says, "Do not let any unwholesome talk come out of your mouths but only what is helpful for building others up" (Eph. 4:29). Harsh language is anything spoken that is belittling, demeaning or cruel.

Harsh language invites one spouse to infer that the other spouse's logic or feelings are dumb or stupid: "That's crazy to think or feel that," "What were you thinking?!" or "If I've told you once, I've told you a thousand times."

Proverbs 18:21 says, "The tongue has the power of life and death." That means that harsh language has sticking power. In one minute of anger, you may say something that your spouse will never forget. Guard your tongue.

3. Retreat

This intruder, retreat, appears when one mate closes the other person out after an argument starts: "End of discussion," "It's over" and "Fine" are all forms of retreat. "Can we talk about this later?" is my retreat intruder of choice. If we were at a meeting of Retreaters Anonymous, this would be the time for me to stand up and say, "Hi. My name is Ted, and I am a retreater. I avoid conflict at any and all costs." Retreat is used by those who just want the conflict to be over; they don't even need resolution to anything. A person who retreats will do or say anything just to make the conflict stop. And all of the unresolved issues are still on the table.

Of all the intruders, this one may not sound so bad to you. You may be thinking, *To walk away and not fight seems healthier than escalating.* That's what I have told myself in the past. It's equally destructive, though, because you are telling your mate that you don't want to hear him or her. My retreat pushes Amy's buttons of disconnection and rejection. When she escalates, all she is doing is raising her word count for the purpose of connecting with me. She, like many women, uses words to connect.

When we argue, I go into the other room away from her. When I leave the room, I disconnect from her not only emotionally but also physically. In her love for me, she follows me into the other room.

After years of working through this, Amy and I have now reached the point where we can resolve most (though not all) conflicts in five to ten minutes. My bent will probably always be to retreat, but now I designate a time to return and reconcile. Fellow retreaters, hear me well: Give your spouse the hope of reconciliation. Designate a time to return. Also, do something constructive with the retreat period: Pray—re-accept the job of your spiritual journey.

4. Assumption

Assumption creeps into a marriage whenever we begin to assign motives to another person's actions. For example, if your spouse comes home late, you may begin to develop negative and false beliefs about what is going on. Your imagination may begin to picture the worst—rather than the best—in your spouse. Assigning motives to your spouse's actions is toxic for a marriage.

A late spouse may reason that there was heavy traffic or the boss called a late meeting. But in a marriage recovering from the aftereffects of an affair, such a reason will more than likely mean, "I was with that other person."

Assumption says things like, "I know what you are thinking and you are wrong," "You did that on purpose," "You are trying to ruin this marriage" or "You do not want me to be successful at my job—that is why you get mad every time I am late."

The conversation can quickly escalate:

"You're late again, and I'm tired of this," the wife says.

"Honey, my job is overwhelming right now," the husband replies.

"When is this going to stop?" the wife asks.

"I don't know," the husband snips.

And suddenly, assumption sneaks in:

Her Mind	His Mind
"He loves his job more than me."	"Doesn't she know the bills we have to pay?"
"We never should have had kids."	"She has no idea what it takes to keep my boss happy."
"Is he losing interest in me?"	"She wants me to quit and stay home all day."

All of these are assumptions. Like an intruder breaking into a secure home, assumptions quickly compromise the marriage. The spousal conflict has nothing to do with kids, bills, sexual interest or quitting. It has to do with the messages of the heart, Level 6 communication. You must get out of your head and into your mate's heart.

QMR, or the Last 10 Percent

Amy and I have developed something in our marriage to help rid our relationship of assumptions. We call it QMR—Quarterly Marriage Realignment. We have one several times a year, usually after I have retreated on an unresolved issue. Pastor Bill Hybels from Willow Creek Church uses the term "the Last 10 Percent," because in conflict, we generally share 90 percent of the problem with little blood, sweat or tears; but the last 10 percent is the elephant in the room—the part that leaves the relationship at risk.

Our last QMR took place at the Branson Landing two months ago. Mondays are our day off from the church. On Tuesday mornings, Amy and I leave the house for breakfast together at 6:30 A.M. On this particular morning we were silent, knowing that we needed to have a hard heart-to-heart conversation—we were headed for the last 10 percent.

Amy and I are at a crossroads in our ministry where we know God is directing us to concentrate on marriage and family ministry, but we were the first two staff members to start Woodland Hills Church five years ago, and we know we still are called there. How do we do both full-time marriage and family ministry *and* church ministry? That was the central question of our QMR. I am Amy's husband, lover and senior pastor. That is the platform of our QMR. Amy is allowed to say things to me that most children's directors cannot say to their senior pastors. The QMR went like this:

"Are you mad?" I have such a way with words, and my timing can be impeccable.

"No, I'm not mad," Amy responded.

"We've both been awfully silent this morning. Do we need to discuss anything?" I asked.

"Where are you at with the church? Do you still want to pastor Woodland Hills?" Amy asked.

That pushed my button of failure. I interpreted her question to mean that I was doing a bad job (assumption intruder).

"What's that supposed to mean?" I asked.

(Notice, all we are doing is asking questions. That is a tell-tail sign that we are in a defensive posture.)

"Well, you didn't seem to be passionate about the content of the staff meeting this morning. Do you even want to move forward with the church and this new vision?" she asked.

Amy and her team had just attended a conference at North Point Church in Atlanta, Georgia, where they were challenged to transition the whole church to a family model of ministry. (Sharing your conference excitement with someone who didn't attend makes the other person often feel like that old "You had to be there" punch line of a great story.) I was excited about the concept that I had learned about three days prior, but I did not share Amy's level of enthusiasm. She was still on the "conference high."

I proceeded with one of the dumbest things I have ever said in my life: "I am the senior pastor." I said it with the same maturity and force as when I was six and declared, "This is my Evel Knievel motorcycle and if you don't stop, I'm taking it and going home!" What a fool I was and still can be!

That shut Amy down. It communicated that I didn't want to be pressured and we were done talking. The next 15 minutes were silent. Poached eggs over an English muffin never tasted so bad.

After 15 minutes went by, I said, "I'm sorry." There was no response from across the booth. I knew then that this was bad.

It then hit me. "I'm sorry" is too much of a blanket statement. She needed a list of what I was sorry for.

"I'm sorry for shutting down the conversation and invalidating your feelings and enthusiasm about the direction of our church. I'm sorry that I elevated my opinions and feelings above yours (harsh language intruder). Will you forgive me?"

"Yes," she said with tears rolling down her face.

Dang you, Ted, I said to myself.

Amy then reminded me that we are not enemies. We are playing on the same team. We spent the next hour—and the rest of the day for that matter—sharing our hearts. Amy shared with me that she wants to be a great mom more than anything and that she one day wants to turn over the children's ministry to capable leaders and step out. I want that for her, too. I shared with her that I don't want to be a

CEO senior pastor, but I want to teach and help people with real life problems, not the organization or structure of the church. She wants that for me, too.

It took a QMR to put aside our assumptions and help us focus on the heart. Focusing on the heart made us immediate teammates.

If you are interested in practicing the QMR or the Last 10 Percent, here are a few guidelines:

1. *Keep it short and simple.* Start by asking permission to share. Let your spouse know, "I need to share with you the Last 10 Percent."

2. *Keep the focus on the relationship, not the issue.* The Last 10 Percent is not to be shared with waiters, cashiers or people you meet on the street. The Last 10 Percent is meant for your close relationships and is a tool to help you work through conflict. Keep in mind that conflict is a valuable crossroads to deeper intimacy. Relationships are more important than opinions.

3. *Keep it face to face.* Never share the Last 10 Percent in an email or over the phone.

What is the real issue that is driving all of the conflict in your marriage? The Bible says, "What causes fights and quarrels among you? Don't they come from your desires that battle within you?" (Jas. 4:1). Here is the source of your conflict in a nutshell: You have a sin nature and so does your mate. You are one imperfect, fallen person married to another imperfect, fallen person—because of the grace of God, your marriage is staying together. The Bible says that "God opposes the proud but gives grace to the humble" (Jas. 4:6). He wants to work in your marriage but only if you'll let Him. You can't keep fixing it yourself. The grace He wants to give you comes only from Him. Yet this grace can only come to those who know they are not perfect and who understand that God is the only One who can change a human heart. And that includes your mate's heart.

Handling Conflict in the Bedroom

Did you know that even Solomon and his bride faced conflict? And one of their biggest conflicts was over the issue of sex! In Song of Songs 5:2, the young bride says, "I slept but my heart [Solomon] was awake. Listen! My lover is knocking: 'Open to me, my sister, my darling, my dove, my flawless one.'"

In other words, Solomon is saying that he's ready to have sex. He's calling her sweet names to get her attention. In modern terms, he's knocking at the door saying, "My dumpling, my sugar, my baby."

The young bride responds in verse 3, "I have taken off my robe— must I put it on again? I have washed my feet—must I soil them again?" This is the equivalent of a Hebrew headache. She's saying, "I'm not in the mood."

And maybe that's fair. Her shepherd king has been gone all day. We know he didn't have access to a cell phone or email, so he hasn't been letting her know throughout the day how much he loves her. Instead, he knocks on her door and asks her to open herself up to him. He wants to have sex with her. She says no. It's their first conflict—and it's over sex.

So if you experience conflict in your marriage and in your sex life, know that you're not alone. Fortunately, there are some ways to handle it well.

Song of Songs 5:4 says, "My lover thrust his hand through the latch-opening; my heart began to pound for him. I arose to open for my lover, and my hand dripped with myrrh." Solomon reached through the door and offered liquid myrrh, which is a sign of sweetness. Notice that he didn't keep pounding.

> *Insanity is doing the same thing over and over again, expecting different results.*

Nowhere in the Bible do we find that arguing, screaming or the silent treatment provides any sort of solution for conflict. Those things simply don't work. God has not empowered you to change your spouse's heart. He has kept all that power to Himself. Instead, He invites you to love, serve and reflect Himself to the person you married.

After Solomon offers his wife myrrh, he walks away. Do you know what happens next? The Scripture says that when he leaves, she starts to want him! Song of Songs 5:6 says, "I opened for my lover, but my lover had left; he was gone. My heart sank at his departure. I looked for him but did not find him. I called him but he did not answer."

Insanity is doing the same thing over and over again expecting different results. For years you may have reacted in the exact same way when your spouse declined an invitation for sexual intimacy. Try a new approach. Respond rather than react.

When Solomon removed himself from the situation, along with any pressure or coercion, God began to work on her heart. This is a young couple in conflict, but both have been fighting fairly. There are no signs of belittling, sarcasm or abuse. They're just having a fight.

How else could Solomon have dealt with this? Some alternative, bad reactions may have sounded like this:

"You're never in the mood."

"You always use the 'I'm tired' excuse."

"We haven't had any in weeks."

Those sweet nothings are sure to get your wife in the mood! Such reactions will simply shut her down. When he walks away, Solomon displays maturity, respect and honor toward his new bride.

The Antidote to Conflict

The antidote to conflict is simple but powerful: forgiveness. When we choose to forgive—and I mean really forgive—we move our focus from what separates us to what brings us together. One of the biggest reasons that Amy and I can survive conflict—whether it's over snorkeling or anything else going on in our marriage—is that we have slammed the door on divorce. We have made the decision that it is not an option for us. In Song of Songs 6:3, the young bride refers to their covenant when she says, "I am my lover's and my lover is mine."

In order to honor our covenant to each other, we have to learn to forgive. Forgiveness is powerful. It's an amazing antidote to selfishness. When you choose to forgive, you can't help but forget about yourself. You give up the right to be right. You will only be able to offer forgiveness to the point at which you understand it, and the greatest understanding of forgiveness comes from God. You and I do not generate one ounce of love. We do not generate one ounce of forgiveness. Love and forgiveness are given to us by God. We love because He first loved us.

You and I do not generate one ounce of love. We do not generate one ounce of forgiveness. Love and forgiveness are given to us by God. We love because He first loved us.

Over the years I've learned a lot about forgiveness—not just in my relationship with Amy, but in all of my relationships both personal and professional. I've learned that there's a big difference between *reconciliation* and *conciliation*. Reconciliation means bringing things back to the way they were. Conciliation means ending things on friendly terms.

Do you know what most couples want today? They don't want reconciliation when they are offering forgiveness—they want conciliation. They want to just go ahead and end the argument without dealing with the real issues, without treasure hunting to discover what's really going on in the other person's heart. Sadly, some even choose divorce—a form of conciliation—because things may end "friendly" (unless, of course, you're one of the kids).

The best possible relationships involve reconciliation—true forgiveness—and as you'll read next, there's nothing better after forgiveness than make-up sex!

Resolving Conflict Enhances Intimacy

When you resolve conflict in your marriage, intimacy is a natural result. The best marriages and relationships cultivate a spirit of forgiveness. Do you know how to have the spirit of forgiveness? Tap into the Source of all forgiveness. If you are not a forgiving person, you don't truly understand how much God has forgiven you. If you walk around as a judgmental person, pride has gripped your heart. You're blinded to your own shortcomings. When you know and recognize your weaknesses and learn to give yourself grace, then you can extend it to others.

And nothing prepares a couple for the bedroom quite like forgiveness. In Song of Songs 6:11-12, the bride says, "I went down to the grove of nut trees to look at the new growth in the valley, to see if the vines had budded or the pomegranates were in bloom. Before I realized it, my desire [Solomon] set me among the royal chariots of my people." In other words, after their conflict, she is restored to a higher place than she was before. That's the power of forgiveness.

Three Ways to Get in the Mood

1. Remember Your Commitment
When you're not in the mood, remember your commitment. I often tell those in pre-marriage counseling that if you're not prepared to have sex two to three times a week, then you don't need to get married. Sex is a key part of marriage. So remember your commitment: You no longer own your body. That means that the guy who is struggling with masturbation must keep in mind that his wife owns his body as well. We are to honor and adore one another.

2. Remember that Sexual Interest Builds
You can probably share stories of times you weren't in the mood, but after you got started, you got in the mood.

There have been plenty of days in our marriage when neither Amy nor I were in the mood. Yes, even as a guy I have those days when sex feels like too much work. Long hours at work, sick kids, all-day baseball tournaments with your kids in 90-degree heat and even camping can hinder the mood. It is on those nights that Amy and I look at each other while brushing our teeth and say, "You know it has been a week."

It surprises both of us how quickly we get in the mood after we get started. Sexual interest truly builds.

3. Remember that It's Not About You

This is important for the husband *and* the wife, but women often feel that it falls on their shoulders. After all, we just talked to ladies a couple of chapters prior to this about the benefits of quickies.

When your goal in sex becomes the pleasure of your spouse, then you truly live out the reality, "It is better to give than to receive" (see Acts 20:35).

Good Conflict Resolution

During that snorkeling expedition on our honeymoon, Amy and I faced all kinds of challenges, including those intruders—escalation, harsh language, retreat and assumption. But do you know what? We worked our way through the conflict. (If you have ever been on a cruise, you know that you usually share a dinner table with two or three other couples. We worked through our issues with a couple from Boston and a couple from Maryland.)

Our solution to the snorkeling fiasco during our honeymoon was not all that profound—our commitment to work through conflict in our marriage was. The act of working through conflict is more important than the outcome or solution. To this day, 11 years later, I honestly don't care what we decide on issues, so long as I know we are both deeply understood and honored. Now we fight over letting the other person win. Weird, I know. Amazing how that works.

Conflict is a valuable crossroads in a relationship. Conflict is good because the make-up is so much sweeter. Did you know that make-up sex is biblical? Do you want to know the two verses I use all the time in our home and I share them in front of my kids? They are "Rejoice in the wife of your youth" (Prov. 5:18) and "Always let her breasts satisfy you" (Prov. 5:19, *GWT*).

So now that you know the intruders of intimacy—and how to resolve conflict—you need to learn about the predators of intimacy. You'll discover that and more in the next chapter.

From GarySmalley.com

Q: My wife is very sensitive and she says that I am not. She feels my apologies are obligatory and not heartfelt. When I hurt her feelings, I want to make it right but often fumble over my words. How can I apologize and convince her I mean it?

A: Here are just a few thoughts for crafting great apologies:

1. *Put some thought into it.* "There is more hope for a fool than for someone who speaks without thinking" (Prov. 29:20, *NLT*). The other person will know the sincerity of your apology by the amount of thought you have given to it.

2. *Focus on her feelings, not the issues.* "We know that we all possess knowledge. Knowledge puffs up, but love builds up" (1 Cor. 8:1). Resolution focuses on the issue, but reconciliation focuses on the relationship. Let your wife know that your marriage is more important than the disagreement.

3. *Become a great wordsmith.* Pick great, meaningful words. "Pleasant words are a honeycomb, sweet to the soul and healing to the bones" (Prov. 16:24). "Reckless words pierce like a sword, but the tongue of the wise brings healing" (Prov. 12:18). "A gentle answer turns away wrath, but a harsh word stirs up anger" (Prov. 15:1).

4. *Remember that less is often more.* Sometimes in our apologies we can bring up three new issues as we try to make amends over one. "Fire goes out for lack of fuel" (Prov. 26:20, *NLT*). "Don't talk too much, for it fosters sin. Be sensible and turn off the flow" (Prov. 10:19, *NLT*). "A man of knowledge uses words with restraint, and a man of understanding is even-tempered. Even a fool is thought wise if he keeps silent, and discerning if he holds his tongue" (Prov. 17:27-28).

Hopefully these tips and Scriptures will help you move from repetitive and programmed apologies to meaningful and heartfelt ones.

Summary

Sometimes little things that impede intimacy can creep into our marriages. Solomon calls these intruders "foxes": "Catch for us the foxes, the little foxes that ruin the vineyards, our vineyards that are in bloom" (Song of Songs 2:15). They are *escalation, harsh language, retreat* and *assumption*.

Insanity is doing the same thing over and over again and expecting different results.

The antidote to conflict is simple but powerful: forgiveness.

When you resolve conflict in your marriage, intimacy is a natural result.

Pillow Talk

Which intruder is your most common defense mechanism in our conflicts?

What can we do to chase these intruders out of our marriage?

Are there any "foxes" loose right now that I need to seek forgiveness for?

CHAPTER 12

The Predators that Ruin the Best Sex of Your Life

Erma and Fred were on a budget because Erma had a little problem with shopping. She came home one afternoon, and Fred was sitting in the chair reading the newspaper. She looked around the corner and said, "Fred, I have a surprise for you."

He looked up over his glasses. "What did you buy?"

"Just close your eyes—it's a surprise," she responded. After Fred reluctantly shut his eyes, Erma came from around the corner and sang with glee, "Ta-*da!*"

"Erma, what did you do?" Fred asked.

"Do you like it? Do you think it looks good?" she responded.

"How much did it cost? Just tell me!" he insisted.

"Doesn't it go great with these shoes?"

"Erma, what did it cost?"

Finally she conceded and told him the cost of the dress.

"What were you thinking? What was going through your mind when you were in the store?"

"Well, I went in the dressing room and I tried on the dress. I looked in the mirror, and the devil just made me buy it. It just looked so good."

"Why didn't you just tell the devil to get behind you?" Fred asked.

"I did, and he said it looked good from back there, too!"

As humorous as this is, the story doesn't have a happy ending. Fred was preoccupied with one of the girls at his office—he couldn't get her off of his mind. Erma's heart was soon broken by the news of his affair.

Sexual temptation is increasingly prevalent and is changing our society and country for the worse. The strength of any country is the family unit, a foundation on which parents raise their children in the fear of God—we raise them in the Bible. If you can unravel the family unit, you can weaken a country. That's why protecting your relationship is so important. In this chapter, we're going to reveal the five predators that couples gradually fall prey to before they discover they've gone too far, and we'll share what you can do to guard your relationship and sex life.

The Five Dreaded Sexual Predators

The dreaded sexual predators that are seeking to sabotage your love life and destroy your marriage have five guises. Because it is a truth that both men and women can fall into immorality, we all need to recognize the destroyers and learn how to prevent a fall. It's like Paul says: "We are not unaware of his [the devil's] schemes" (2 Cor. 2:11) and Peter corroborates, "The devil prowls around like a roaring lion looking for someone to devour" (1 Pet. 5:8). While the devil can't take your soul because you are secure with Jesus, he can get you to the point where you are disqualified, distracted and lost. If you look in the Old Testament, you'll see many great leaders who became lost because of immorality. The good news is that once you know the five sexual predators, you can protect yourself and your family from them.

1. The Vacuum of Intimacy Predator

So far, we've learned that intimacy is not just sexual, but it's also emotional. Intimacy means being able to sit with your mate and communicate freely. If you get to a point in your marriage where there is an emotional vacuum—an elimination of intimacy—that void will demand to be filled, and you may experience the deadly sexual predator know as the vacuum of intimacy.

If you become a butler or a maid in a marriage, you have a vacuum of intimacy—the intimacy in the relationship is gone. I (Ted) remember the words of a young lady who said something I'll never forget: "I just wish my husband would treat me as well as he does the waitress when we go out to eat and say 'Please' and 'Thank you' and show some kind of appreciation."

If you aren't satisfying your mate when it comes to intimacy, you can rest assured that the devil has picked out someone right around the corner who will. I promise you he will wag that person in front of your spouse at the most opportune times—and you'll fall prey to this predator.

2. The Fantasy Predator

The sexual predator known as fantasy creeps in when you start building your own Fantasy Island in your imagination: You start picturing yourself with another person. You start thinking about how this other person responds to you, laughs at your jokes and recognizes little things about you that your spouse has either forgotten or has not mentioned. When you want more of this little drug that you have tasted, you become a junky, and you start building a great fantasy life with this person. You start daydreaming, and in the process you invite the second predator into your life: fantasy.

> *The grass is greener on the other side*
> *of the fence because that's where*
> *you're watering with your hose—*
> *or there is a septic leak.*

Now, fantasy may seem harmless at first, but don't be fooled! This predator is deadly. You may start looking on the other side of the fence because the grass is greener over there. But I once heard someone say that the grass is greener on the other side of the fence because that's where you're watering with your hose. Wherever you are watering and feeding with your thoughts is the place that's going to look like Shangri-la, and you are going to think you need to be there. What has happened is your own pasture has dried up and died because you are not feeding and watering it. Where you go with your thoughts will determine which pasture looks the greenest. You naturally want to be where the pasture looks the best.

When facing the fantasy predator, make sure that you take captive every thought to make it obedient to Christ. This is when you have to ask yourself, *What can I do to make my relationship with my spouse better?* In other words, What can you do to make your side of the fence look greener? Start watering your side of the fence with your thoughts. You have to constantly push those impure thoughts out of your head and replace them with godly thoughts. As Paul said, whatever things are lovely, just, pure and praiseworthy, meditate on these things (see Phil. 4:8).

You *can* control your thoughts. The devil doesn't make you do it—you choose what you allow into your mind. You can choose to fight off the predator of fantasy and get back to reality. The good news is that you don't have to do it alone. You can get accountability. You can get encouragement. You can get people around you who will pray for you, love you and challenge you to live pure and holy.

Jesus said, "You have heard that it was said, 'Do not commit adultery.' But I tell you that anyone who looks at a woman lustfully has already committed adultery with her in his heart" (Matt. 5:27-28).

In fact the Bible says a lot about lust and purity:

- Job 31:1 says, "I made a covenant with my eyes not to look lustfully at a girl."

- Psalm 101:3 says, "I will set before my eyes no vile thing."

- 2 Corinthians 10:5 says, "Take captive every thought to make it obedient to Christ."

Whether or not you're married, you will face sexual temptation. Joseph, as a young man, was tempted, and do you know what the Bible says he did? He did what we should all do when faced with the predator fantasy: He sprinted out of there! He would not put himself in that position. He would not stay in that situation where his brain could go. He took off. He ran. (Read Genesis 39 for the whole episode.)

What did Jesus do when He was tempted by the devil three times? He used the Word of God. When you are tempted in your mind, do the same (see Matt. 4:1-11; Luke 4:1-13). When you are tempted in the flesh, run—get out of there. I can't tell you how many people I have counseled who say, "Well, me and my girlfriend really blew it."

I'll ask, "Really? What were you doing?"

"Well, we were alone and started kissing and clothes started coming off."

They wonder why they fell into sin. If you allow the fantasy predator into your life, it won't be long until other predators follow.

3. The Intentional Encounter Predator

You fall prey to the intentional encounter when you, in effect, start building a bridge to Fantasy Island. This is where you start playing with temptation, like Samson did with Delilah. You may already know the biblical story: Samson (whose name means "sun") starts messing with Delilah (whose name means "dangling curls"), and Delilah wraps him around her little finger, eventually snuffing out Samson's light and life. In the end, Samson ends up blinded, binded and grinded. He gets burned. (Read Judges 16:4-22 for the details.)

Intentionally placing yourself in the path of the person who might fill your emotional vacuum is inviting a deadly predator into your marriage relationship. If the person is a coworker, you make sure that you both are at the water cooler or you take a break at the same time. Or you work extra-long days when just you two are in the office. If it's a waiter or waitress, you find out that person's shift so that you can be there. You make sure you are at the right place at the right time, and in the process you fall prey to the intentional encounter predator. We like what our friend Dr. Gary Chapman says about intentional encounters at the water cooler: "If this is a problem for you at work, stop drinking water altogether. If that lady ever leaves your workplace, then you can start drinking water again."

Here is where it gets very dangerous. Proverbs 7:6-9 says, "At the window of my house I looked out through the lattice. I saw among the simple, I noticed among the young men, a youth who lacked judgment. He was going down the street near her corner, walking along in the direction of her house at twilight, as the day was fading, as the dark of night set in." In other words, this young man was putting himself in a place where he knew he was going to have that encounter again. He was going down the street near her corner, walking along the direction of her house at twilight as the day was fading. What time of day was it? Where was he? He was in the red-light district.

Proverbs 7 continues, "Then out came a woman to meet him, dressed like a prostitute and with crafty intent. (She is loud and defiant, her feet never stay at home)" (vv. 10-11). There is no fear of God in this woman. She has made a covenant of marriage and it's irrelevant to her. It doesn't mean anything.

"(Now in the street, now in the squares, at every corner she lurks.) She took hold of him and kissed him and with a brazen face she said: 'I have fellowship offerings at home; today I have fulfilled my vows'" (vv. 12-14). She's basically saying, "I'm a Christian, so it's okay. I have a fish on the back of my car. Listen: You're not happy with your marriage and you're not happy with your spouse, so let's get together." Sadly, we have seen more people than we can count who say that God spoke to them and told them to divorce their mate. Yet when these deceived people are asked, "Oh really? For what reason?" the answer is usually the same—because they're not happy.

I (Gary) can remember how very close I once came to cheating on Norma. We had three kids. I was busy at work and lonely on the road. I was overworked and tired. If that wasn't enough, I also had easy access to hotels because of my travel schedule—and before I knew it, I noticed myself working late with a particular woman.

One night while trying to finish a project for my boss, this woman and I worked late into the night. Because it was late, we ended up working in my hotel room. The project was due in two days, and I couldn't get it done alone—or at least that's what I thought at the time. I was literally burning inside with desire.

Though I never once inappropriately touched her, I let my imagination go free. I must have had sex with her a hundred times in my mind. Years later, she admitted she might have fallen if I had pursued her then.

When I think back on that night, I still remember the war that raged inside of me: The thought of hurting Norma and my kids. The thought I might be rejected. The thought of falling away from God. The thought of disgracing the ministry God had called me to. The thought of all the consequences I had heard from other couples who had been torn apart by an affair. All these thoughts bombarded me at once.

And the image that stuck in my mind most of all was looking at my three kids with their saddened eyes as they and Norma walked out of my life. It was too much.

Little did I know that I could have had sexual freedom back then but didn't know how to get it. I didn't know about hiding the Word in my heart and how that could set me free from sexual temptation.

4. The Expression Predator

Suppose you have crossed over the bridge to Fantasy Island. You unload your heart. Your expressions are like verbal tennis, and phone calls or emails sound like this:

"I sure like spending time with you."

"Me, too."

"It's just so much better when I'm with you than it is with my spouse."

"Yeah—me, too. Mine doesn't make me feel this way."

"Neither does mine."

You go back and forth with this verbal tennis, and now you have done everything except the act. When you meet this expression predator—when you start unloading your heart and get affirmation from the other person—your marriage relationship is almost over.

In Proverbs 6:27, Solomon says, "Can a man scoop fire into his lap without his clothes being burned?" If you start playing in this area, you will get burned. You may be tempted to argue that the person makes you feel good or alive, or the person makes you feel like your spouse never did. But you made a covenant with God Almighty, and God does not take lightly vows that are broken.

5. The Acting Out Predator

After you have expressed your heart, you become susceptible to the predator known as acting out; it's just a matter of getting alone or finding someplace to experience each other. There is great danger here. The ramifications of this one decision—which may feel good at the time—are beyond your wildest comprehension. That's why I always advise: Look past the pleasure to the pain. Look to your Savior, Lord Jesus

Christ. Then look to the people closest to you—your spouse, your children, your family, your coworkers, your neighbors. You will hurt them all. You will damage their trust, their faith, their beliefs and their hearts.

In my (Gary's) book *The Language of Love: How to Be Instantly Understood by Those You Love*, I share the story of a young lady who writes her daddy a letter. He has left his family for another woman. One day, he checks the mail at his new home and opens a letter from his daughter:

Dear Daddy,

It's late at night and I'm sitting in the middle of my bed writing to you. I have wanted to talk to you so many times during the past few weeks, but there never seems to be any time when we are alone. Dad, I realize you are dating someone else and I know you and Mom may never get back together. That is terribly hard to accept, especially knowing that you may never come back home or be an everyday dad to me and Brian again.

At least I want you to understand what is going on in our lives. Don't think that Mom asked me to write this, she didn't. She doesn't know I am writing and neither does Brian. I just want to share with you what I have been thinking. Dad, I feel like our family has been riding in a nice car for a long time. You know the kind you always liked to have as a company car; the kind that has every extra inside and not a scratch on the outside.

Over the years the car has developed some problems. It's smoking a lot, the wheels wobble and the seat covers are ripped. The car has been really hard to drive or ride in because of all its shaking and squeaking, but it is still a great automobile, or at least it could be with a little work. I know it could run for years. Since we got the car, Brian and I have been in the back seat while you and Mom have been up front. We feel really secure with you driving and Mom beside you.

But last month, Mom was at the wheel. It was nighttime and we had just turned the corner near our house. Suddenly, we all looked up and saw another car out of control, heading straight for us. Mom tried to swerve out of the way, but the other car still smashed into us. The impact sent us flying off the road and crashing into a lamppost. The thing is, Dad, just before being hit, we could see that you were the one driving the other car. We saw something else; sitting next to you was another woman.

It was such a terrible accident that we were all rushed to the emergency room. But when we asked where you were, no one knew. We are still not really sure where you are or if you were hurt or if you need help. Mom was really hurt. She was thrown into the steering wheel and broke several ribs. One of them punctured her lungs and almost pierced her heart. When the car wrecked, the back door smashed into Brian and he was covered with cuts from the broken glass and he shattered his arm, which is now in a cast. But that is not the worst. He is still in so much pain and shock that he doesn't want to talk or play with anyone. As for me, I was thrown from the car. I was stuck out in the cold for a long time with my right leg broken. As I lay there, I couldn't move and didn't know what was wrong with Mom or Brian. I was hurting so much myself that I couldn't help them.

There have been times since that night when I wondered if any of us would make it. Even though we are getting a little better, we are still in the hospital. The doctors say I will need a lot of therapy on my leg and I know they can help me get better, but I wish it was you who was helping me instead of them. The pain is so bad, but what is even worse is that we all miss you so much. Every day we wait to see if you are going to visit us in the hospital and every day you don't come. I know it is over, but my heart would explode with joy if somehow I could look up and see you walk into my room. At night when the hospital is really quiet, they push Brian and me into Mom's room and we all talk about you. We talk about how much we love driving with you and how we wish you were with us now.

Are you all right? Are you hurting from the wreck? Do you need us like we need you? If you need me, I am here and I love you.

Your daughter,
Kimberly[1]

Always look past the pleasure to the pain. Sin is fun for a brief season, and then Satan runs off laughing when you fall. I want to give you one thing that you can do as a married couple that will make sure this doesn't happen to you in your marriage. If you will do this one thing, you will fill the emotional vacuum and 95 percent of the time the problem will be fixed.

It's one word: *date*. I'll make it two words: *date night*. Make it a non-negotiable.

From GarySmalley.com

Q: *I work in an office where I am quite tempted. How do I fight sexual temptation in the workplace?*

A: Set high standards and guidelines for yourself and keep to them.

Here is a list my pastor, Ted Cunningham, shared with the congregation a few weeks ago. He has adapted this list from Pastor Rick Warren's list for his pastoral staff at Saddleback Church in California. Take this list and make it your own. Make it fit your work environment. Discuss it with your boss. Talk about it with your spouse.

1. Thou shalt not go to lunch alone with the opposite sex. (Parishioners over 65 are okay. Please don't ask me why I arbitrarily picked that age. It's not meant to offend anyone.)

2. Thou shalt not have the opposite sex pick you up or drive you places when it's just the two of you.

3. Thou shalt not visit the opposite sex alone at home.

4. Thou shalt keep the door open when counseling the opposite sex alone, and thou shalt not counsel the opposite sex more than once without that person's mate. Refer them.

5. Thou shalt not discuss detailed sexual problems with the opposite sex in counseling. Refer them.

6. Thou shalt not discuss your marriage problems with an attendee of the opposite sex.

7. Thou shalt be careful in answering emails or letters from the opposite sex.

8. Thou shalt allow any staff member access to your computer at a moment's notice to check your browser history.

Do you see points from this list that would work in your workplace? This list can be the start of building great security in your marriage.

I recently worked with a couple who told me that the wife was jealous of her husband traveling out of town on trips with a woman from his office. She thought that it placed her husband in a compromising, tempting situation. Her concern was enough of a reason for him to not go on trips, but he was concerned that he could lose his job if he explained it to his boss. I encouraged him to share the integrity behind his decision. Guarding sex in marriage is very much an integrity issue, not to mention the security it builds into the marriage. He declined the trips and his boss had no problem with his decision. Actually, his boss applauded his decision to honor his wife's request.

Don't put yourselves in situations where you'll be tempted. Get out of situations where you are tempted. "Be careful—watch out for the attacks from Satan, your great enemy. He prowls around like a hungry, roaring lion, looking for some victim to tear apart" (1 Pet. 5:8, *TLB*). Take precautions.

Note
1. Gary Smalley and John Trent, *The Language of Love: How to Be Instantly Understood by Those You Love* (Carol Stream, IL: Tyndale House Publishers, new ed. 2006), p. 20.

Summary

The vacuum of intimacy predator enters a marriage when there is an emotional vacuum—an elimination of intimacy—and that void demands to be filled.

The fantasy predator creeps in when you start picturing yourself with another person.

The intentional encounters predator is when you start arranging your steps to "bump" into the person you are fantasizing about.

When you unload your heart to the other person, you fall prey to the expression predator.

The acting out predator seeks a time and a place to get alone and experience each other. There is great danger here.

Pillow Talk

What safeguards do we have in place right now to keep these predators out?

What are you doing to guard our marriage from outside forces that may try to weaken or undermine our relationship?

Is our marriage safe enough to share with each other when we are tempted by any of these predators?

What is our game plan for fighting and resisting temptation?

Conclusion

On the day that the manuscript for this book was due, the following headline hit the front page of the *Chicago Tribune*: "The 237 Reasons to Have Sex." Reporter Judy Peres stated the following: "If you think people have sex for pleasure and for procreation, you're right. They also have sex to get rid of a headache, to celebrate a special occasion, to get a promotion and to feel closer to God."[1]

I (Ted) devoured the article to see how many of the reasons people gave for having sex line up with what we present in this book. Of the 237 reasons, very few reflect biblical truth—sadly. The article reports the findings of a new survey:

> Most of the students gave the usual reasons for having sex: "I was attracted to the person," "It feels good" and "I wanted to show my affection" were high on the lists of both men and women. Lesser priorities on both lists were reasons such as, "Someone offered me money to do it," "I felt sorry for the person," "I wanted to punish myself" and "Because of a bet."

Our prayer is that this book encourages you to have great sex for all the right reasons.

Great sex is at the end of great lovemaking. Great lovemaking builds honor, security and intimacy first, and then has the freedom to enjoy foreplay, creativity and release.

"Drink your fill, O lovers!"
—*God (Song of Songs 5:1)*

Note

1. Judy Peres, "The 237 Reasons to Have Sex," *The Chicago Tribune*, August 1, 2007. http://www.chicagotribune.com/news/chi-sex01aug01,0,649209.story?page=1&coll=chi-newsopinion-hed (accessed October 2007).

Answers to the Biggies

One sunny afternoon in Branson, Missouri, I (Ted) had the opportunity to take bestselling author and psychologist Kevin Leman fishing in the trophy trout area of Lake Taneycomo. Now Kevin Leman loves fly fishing.

We were casting into the lake when Kevin turned to me and asked, "What month is it?

"April," I answered. "Any particular reason?"

"Statistically, women enjoy sex more in June than any other month of the year," he responded. "I'm just waiting for June."

Maybe you grew up in a church or home that never talked about sex. In my seminars, I've found that about two-thirds of attendees grew up in homes where sex was a guarded topic, meaning it wasn't discussed very much and when it was, there were fake little names for everything. Only about one-third of attendees grew up in homes that were open to discussing sex.

I grew up in one of those silent homes. My parents took the "Q & A" approach to sex: They only addressed the issue if I asked the questions. I remember my mom was washing dishes one night after dinner. I had heard something at school earlier in the day. I went up to her and asked (complete with hand gestures), "Is this how it works?"

"That's exactly how it works, Ted," she replied.

I thought, *Oh, how disgusting! How gross! What are you adults thinking? There's nothing fun about that.*

Or how about my (Gary's) 10-year-old granddaughter, Hannah. "Gramps, when I get married to Kyle, we'll adopt three kids and live in a big house by the lake."

"Oh, really," I replied. "Why are you adopting?"

"Because I'm never doing that nasty thing with him."

That's good! I thought. *Let's keep it that way.*

God designed it, created it and said it is very good. I (Ted) have come a long way. Now I think sex is great. I thoroughly enjoy it. And in premarital counseling, I go out of my way to discuss it.

Perspectives on Sex

People have a lot of questions about sex. There are a few reasons for this, but the main reason is that, as we've said, in a lot of homes and most churches sex is a taboo topic. I remember the first time I taught on sex at Woodland Hills. I was met with some resistance. This was the first time for many of our church family to hear the subject of marital sexual intimacy discussed on a Sunday morning. (Imagine the senior adults grabbing the bulletin and teaching notes that read "Five Keys to a Suc-SEX-ful Marriage.")

Three days after teaching that message, I was walking through an office building in downtown Branson when I was invited into Adam's (one of our members) office for an impromptu meeting.

"Ted, I must tell you how shocked I was with your talk on Sunday," he said. "As you started the message, I was floored at the inappropriateness of the topic."

"Okay." That was all I could say.

"My wife and I left church and spent the entire afternoon talking about the morning," he continued.

I was bracing myself to hear that Adam and his family would be leaving our church because of the sermon, but he surprised me.

"Our afternoon conversation was followed by the best sex we have ever had—and we have been married for over 20 years. So keep up the good work!"

I still smile when I think of that conversation. Because sex isn't discussed in the Church very often, there's a lot of confusion between what the world, the Church and our parents have taught us and God's perspective on sex.

Beliefs the World Has Taught Us:
• If it feels good, do it.
• We can't control ourselves.
• People are objects.

Beliefs the Church and Our Parents Have Taught Us:
· Sex is bad or dirty.
· Sex should not be talked about. Let's talk about my funeral instead. (In the end, neither is talked about.)

God's Perspective on Sex

Look at Adam and Eve in the garden, enjoying a perfect relationship with God. The Bible says that they "were both naked, and they felt no shame" (Gen. 2:25). This meant that every thought in Adam's mind of his wife's naked body was pure, as was Eve's every thought of Adam's body. Their sexuality was holy. It was something of beauty. It was the most enjoyable thing that God gave two people to experience.

When they ate from the tree, when they committed that act of disobedience, the Bible says that "the eyes of both of them were opened, and they realized they were naked" (Gen. 3:7). They "made coverings for themselves" by sewing fig leaves together (Gen. 3:7).

Now here is my question to you: *Why did they do that?*

I can understand hiding from God because of shame from disobedience. But why did they cover that which was beautiful and pure to each other? I sometimes wonder if it was because for the first time—now that man was sinful—Adam had a perverse, twisted thought about his wife's sexuality. There's no telling what went through his mind, but evidently, he now had an impure thought about his wife's nakedness. And he probably thought that if he had those thoughts about her, what's she thinking about him? So they covered up their nakedness.

Then God asked Adam, "Where are you?" (Gen. 3:9). God knew exactly where they were, but He called to them anyway. God pursued them. He was the hound of heaven. When Adam answered, God asked, "Who told you that you were naked?" (Gen. 3:11).

Why does God even mention the nakedness? I don't know, but I think that's why a lot of people in the Church have a hard time when we start talking about sexuality. Our flesh is fallen. We know that what God originally made beautiful, holy and pure is now twisted in our fallen world.

Throughout this book, we've given you the tools you need to have the best sex of your life. But we realize that there are probably some questions you still have. In this appendix, we want to explore some of the big questions about sex, including frequency, oral sex and masturbation. We've divided it into different sections with the most common questions people ask. If you have a question that's not addressed here, we'd love to hear from you at the Smalley Relationship Center. Simply visit www.GarySmalley.com or www.TedCunningham.com and email us your question!

Questions About Premarital Sex

Can We Have Sex If We Are Planning on Getting Married?

Hebrews 13:4 says, "Marriage should be honored by all, and the marriage bed kept pure for God will judge the adulterer and all the sexually immoral." Sex was designed for marriage. It wasn't designed to be outside of marriage. Within the boundaries of marriage is where you are going to enjoy sex to the fullest.

God wants us to become like Jesus, to become *sanctified*. That is a big word, but it just means to get all the earthly stuff out of you and become more like Jesus. When you become born again, the Holy Spirit dwells in you and you become a body of Christ, or a part of the Body. Paul views any type of sex outside of marriage as prostitution. When you have sexual intercourse, you become one flesh. That is the idea of sex first and foremost: to become one—unity.

Remember that Solomon told us to guard our heart above all else. Our beliefs take residence within our hearts. Even before marriage, our advice is to purify your heart with salvation through Christ, with His Word hidden within your heart and with the power of His Holy Spirit alive and penetrating every corner of your heart. Being free from the continual lust of the flesh is to enter marriage with the power to say no to the lust of another man or woman and yes enthusiastically to your bride or groom. Just imagine spending your honeymoon on some exotic beach with eyes just for your new loved one. You'll have the freedom to please your mate in every way and serve him or her in creativity. You can focus your pleasurable "lust" on one person to the max and give God the glory for creating sex and keeping it for one person.

What If We Are Already Having Sex and Planning on Getting Married?
We know that God forgives. Let these verses seep into your heart:

> What happiness for those whose guilt has been forgiven! What joys when sins are covered over! What relief for those who have confessed their sins and God has cleared their record (Ps. 32:1-2, *TLB*).

> You will never succeed in life if you try to hide your sins. Confess them and give them up; then God will show mercy to you (Prov. 28:13, *GNT*).

> No matter how deep the stain of your sins, I can take it out and make you as clean as freshly fallen snow (Isa. 1:18, *TLB*).

> All have sinned; . . . yet now God declares us "not guilty" if we trust in Jesus Christ, who . . . freely takes away our sins (Rom. 3:23-24, *TLB*).

> There is no condemnation for those who live in union with Christ Jesus (Rom. 8:1).

> Christ can give you a fresh start. Yes, it is worth it to stop now, even if you are getting married next month or next week. You'll be glad you did!

How Long Do We Need to Date Before We Get Married?
One of my (Ted's) greatest encouragements for young couples is to take it slow. In Genesis 29, Jacob falls in love with Rachel. The Bible says he was smitten with this young lady. He did something different from what I did on my first date with my future wife: He kissed her. He then committed to work for her father for seven years in order to be able to marry her. Jacob actually served 14 years, because Rachel's father pulled one over on him. Jacob first married the oldest daughter, Leah, and then served seven more years before he could marry Rachel. But the Bible says that the first seven years "seemed like only a few days to him because of his love for her," so it can be safely assumed that the second seven years passed the same way.

I've seen a lot of marriages where the opposite is true. Instead of years feeling like days, days feel like years. That's often because people were in a rush to get married.

I encourage teens and young adults to make mistakes while dating. Now hear me: I am not talking about making moral failures. I'm talking about learning and growing. Practice communication. Practice resolving conflict. Practice purity. Practice loving someone, even when they're unlovable. Some of the best relationship lessons are learned while dating.

When those lessons aren't learned, couples are put in a tough situation. I've had more than one couple come in for premarital counseling when they were almost done with the wedding plans; and as we talked through issues, it became apparent that the couple was not ready to get married. And I wasn't afraid to let them know that. They'll usually respond, "Are you kidding?! Do you know how much we have already spent for this thing?!" I tell them divorces are far more expensive than the $10,000 to $25,000 they'll spend on the wedding.

Spending money is not a reason to get married. It's better to reschedule or call it off. In the old days, people went to a pastor to seek permission to marry and see if they were ready. But now people just want their spiritual leader to conduct and bless the ceremony.

Don't rush marriage. Time is your best friend. Don't treat it as the enemy. Time allows infatuation to fade. Time allows the warm fuzzies to get old. You're probably thinking that you don't want them to get old, but time buys you the opportunity to get sound biblical direction for your life and to discover whether this person is right or wrong for you.

Can I Marry Someone Who Isn't a Believer?

Willingly going into a marriage knowing as a believer that you are marrying someone who does not profess Christ as his or her Lord and Savior is prohibited in the Bible. In 2 Corinthians 6, Paul says, "Do not be yoked together with unbelievers. For what do righteousness and wickedness have in common? Or what fellowship can light have with darkness? What harmony is there between Christ and Belial? What does a believer have in common with an unbeliever?" (vv. 14-15).

Now 1 Peter 3:1-6 provides wisdom and encouragement to a wife who is married to an unbeliever. The passage says not to leave him, preach at him or nag him, but with "a gentle and quiet spirit" live out your faith before him (v. 4). That kind of faith is not only "of great worth" to God, but can also actually win the husband over (see v. 1).

For the person married to an unbeliever, there is hope. I have heard spouses at our church say they've tried everything. They've turned up the local Christian radio station extra loud. They've left their Bible on their spouse's pillow. They've tried overt acts of evangelizing. But the Bible says the most effective thing you can do is live out your faith. I've watched as women in our church have taken this approach. It usually isn't too long until the husband comments, "She's starting to rub off on me."

If We Are Engaged and Know that We're Going to Get Married, Why Can't We Go Ahead and Live Together?

The Bible prohibits cohabitation. The Bible says, "Flee from sexual immorality. All other sins a man commits are outside his body, but he who sins sexually sins against his own body" (1 Cor. 6:18).

Ask yourself this simple question: *How free am I to wait for sex in marriage?* Now rate yourself from 1 to 10.

Have no patience	1 2 3 4 5 6 7 8 9 10	Have healthy anticipation
Fantasize every day	1 2 3 4 5 6 7 8 9 10	Know he/she is worth it
Masturbate regularly	1 2 3 4 5 6 7 8 9 10	Trust God in this area

If you're a man, a score of 10 would show itself by being free to love all women in the sense that you are hoping that they have someone to love them as God intended. If you're thinking about undressing them in your mind and lying with them for your pleasure, you don't have God's heart yet and you don't have the beliefs in your heart that reflect His words.

If you say to yourself, *I always hope they are being cared for by a loving dad, husband or friend,* then you're thinking about their greater good rather than your own sinful desires.

I love what Dr. Richard Dobbins says:

Sometimes when I'm talking to teens, I draw an analogy between the bonding capacity of the body and adhesive tape. Adhesive tape is not made for repetitive use. The strongest bond adhesive tape is capable of making is formed with the first surface to which it is applied. You can remove the tape and reapply it to other surfaces several times, and it will still adhere. However, with every application, some of the adhesiveness has been compromised. Finally, if you continue the practice long enough, there will not be enough adhesiveness left to make the tape stick to any surface. God intended that the bond between mates be the closest and strongest one they are capable of forming. That is why Paul makes it very clear that the body is not for fornication.[1]

Do you understand the analogy? Oneness is affected when you give a piece of yourself away. The media often tries to tell us that sex is nothing more than a quick exchange. But sex is so much more—not just a physical consummation but also all of the other levels of connection. When you sleep with someone you're not married to, you're giving him or her a piece of yourself, and that undermines God's plan for oneness in marriage.

What Should I Do to Prepare Sexually for My Honeymoon?
I like to tell young people that I think the wedding is the worst thing for the honeymoon—I really do. Don't let your Aunt Sue and Uncle Bob determine what time you have your wedding. They will try to make you feel guilty and shame you into what they want. The wedding is about you. You're the focus. Select a wedding time that works for you. When you get married at 2 P.M., take pictures for three hours, and then dance until midnight, you'll stumble into the hotel room exhausted. You're not going to be fresh for sex!

When I talk to young men, I tell them that they will probably be exhausted on their wedding night. Arousal may come easily, but they may only last 20 to 30 seconds—and then they will be upset with themselves. The good news is that there are exercises young men can practice to prepare for the wedding night that can help them have greater control. Talk to your doctor. Get an examination.

Women often complain that their first night of intercourse is painful and unpleasant—both bride and groom should educate themselves and realize that this is normal. But if couples practice honoring one another, building security and nurturing intimacy in the days leading up to the honeymoon, sex can still be a wonderful experience of connection and fulfillment, even if there is minor discomfort the first few times. (If the bride's discomfort continues for more than a few days, she should see her doctor.)

I remember one couple we counseled before they were married. Both were virgins—they had saved themselves for each other. They were excited about the honeymoon and the wedding and everything else. About two months into their marriage, they were miserable: When they had sex, he would get his, roll over and go to sleep. She never reached orgasm. She was left thinking, *If this is all sex is, forget it.* And he was thinking sex was phenomenal.

I had to counsel him. I had to sit him down one-on-one and teach him how to bring his wife pleasure. He didn't know—no one had ever taught him. She didn't want to have sex with him anymore, so I told him not to make any advances toward her, to wait until she made advances toward him and then do *this* and *this* and *that* to her. I taught him a few things he could do.

He called me in a week and said, "You're a genius."

Questions About Lust and Temptation

What Can I Do to Protect Myself from Lust?

Men tend to lust for physical release or conquest, viewing women as challenges for satisfying their sexual drives. Lust makes us think that having some person we don't presently have would make us happier. Often that person is simply a figment of our imagination. Even if the person is real, we often attach unreal character traits to him or her. Usually our lust focuses on sexual involvement because we imagine that if we had such a person to hold in our arms, it would be exciting and wonderfully fulfilling. Men can, however, also lust for a sporting event and be depressed after a great loss.

Women tend to lust for men other than their husband, especially if their married relationship is strained. But women lust for jewelry, furnishings, houses and a host of other things, as well.

We can all lust for things other than God if our beliefs are strong about gaining the maximum amount of pleasure, fun, excitement and thrills that life can bring us. This is a very normal worldly belief system. The only problem is that if we are friends with the world, we can't be God's friend. We must decide whether or not to take the Giver of Life's friendship over the empty world's beliefs.

I have talked to people that have gone through affairs or are getting ready to get into affairs because of the idea that the grass is greener on the other side. I simply say, "The reason that sounds exciting to you is because you are not raising kids with that person. You are not paying bills with that person. You are not mowing the lawn with that person."

It's easy to think that you can leave one person and go to the next and everything will be better. But that doesn't happen—all your expectations and problems and issues will follow you.

Men are a lot like puppies. Have you ever approached a puppy? When you approach a puppy, your voice goes up an octave or two, and you go, "That's such a good boy." As you're saying those words, guys get excited: Our tails start wagging and we just want you to give us something else to do. We just want to impress you. Remember that men don't think there is a problem with the relationship until you ask us about the relationship. Guys, this should shock us! It should really wake us up that most women would not walk down the aisle with us again.

I can't tell you the number of couples I've counseled who met at a party. Your chances of successfully marrying someone from a party are pretty slim. I am just finding out that booze is a great revealer, not a great concealer, and you are seeing a fun side of a person. When two partiers get married, it usually isn't too long before they wake up to the reality of bills, jobs and kids. The party is over and they begin wondering, *What have I done?* They weren't properly prepared for the commitment of marriage.

So how do you protect yourself from sexual lust? I have found full disclosure with my wife and prayer to be the most successful safeguards from lust. When an attractive woman walks by, the first thing I do is begin to pray for that individual. I assume that every woman I meet has a dad that didn't love her. I think she probably has a husband that doesn't care for her. She probably has a boss that is mean to her. I pray, "Father, may she know what Your love is like today." It's kind of like how we are commanded to treat our enemies. When you are praying for your enemies and wishing good things on them, it's hard to have evil thoughts toward them. It's hard to have a lustful thought toward a woman when you are praying for God's best in her life and God's love in her life.

How Do *You* Deal with Temptation and Lust?

Recently, I (Gary) was out of town and decided to walk two miles along a quiet road. Before long, a beautiful girl wearing the briefest of shorts and skimpiest of halter tops jogged by. After she passed, I asked myself, *Why do I, at 65, still have lustful thoughts? When will I stop being tempted as if I were still 16 years old?* It occurred to me that if all my feelings and actions come from the beliefs in my heart, maybe I have a belief from childhood that's driving my thoughts. I know that if we lack wisdom, we can always ask God. We can talk to Him about anything without feeling embarrassed. So I decided to ask God where my struggle with lust came from.

Within minutes it hit me. I was raised by a father and older siblings who seemed totally focused on seeking pleasure for themselves regardless of the feelings or needs of others around them. Most of their attention was on things like fishing, hunting, movies, food, dating, sex, affairs, gambling, vacations, water sports, skiing or anything that would bring the greatest amount of pleasure or power. So I grew up with the basic belief instilled in me that life was about my personal pleasure and gratification. Without even being aware of it, this belief crept into my heart.

Scriptures began flashing through my mind that taught the very opposite. One of them was Galatians 5:13: "You, my brothers, were called to be free. But do not use your freedom to indulge the sinful nature; rather, serve one another in love." My freedom in Christ was not given to enable me to pursue sexual or exciting pleasures but rather to serve others by loving them in the same way that I wanted to be loved. The focus was not to be on me and my gratification but on the good of other people. Instead of serving myself, I get to serve others.

When we adopt the attitude that we are here to serve, just as Christ was, all areas of our lives will be affected. As I walked that morning, I repeated Galatians 5:13 over and over again in my mind, working the principle of service into my heart to replace the selfishness of lustful thoughts. Day after day, I began to think more about serving others through love than about using others for my pleasure. As I focused on changing my beliefs by hiding God's Word in my heart, I was amazed by how fast my actions changed naturally. Within two weeks of memorizing this verse and repeating it back to God from morning until night, lustful thoughts began to disappear. Now when a lustful thought starts to move toward me, I simply say to God, "I used to be a hedonist, Lord, but You have given me the power to serve others through Your love." Instead of fantasizing about some girl, I imagine just how much God loves her. And I hope she reads this book someday in order to discover God's best for her life.

How Far Do I Go in Discussing This Lust Problem with My Wife?

Discuss tendencies, not details. When my (Ted's) wife, Amy, learned about the male brain (as explored in chapter 4), it was one of the best things that ever happened in our marriage and in my life. I want her to know what tempts me. Before I head out for a weekend speaking trip, Amy will say, "I am going to get you good and sexed up so you will not struggle with temptation and lust." Many of my send-offs for trips are quickies.

If you do discuss this problem with your mate, explain how you are seeking God's ways to overcome it. Ladies, your husband lusts or he is tempted to lust—or he has another problem. But as soon as God begins to give him the same freedom I've seen within my coauthor, Gary, you will see an amazing change in your husband's life. Most men lust—that's a fact. Now the question is, Do you want to know those details? The answer should be no. Your husband should have a man who will hold him accountable. He can share the specifics of those struggles with the other man in a healthy relationship. I once knew a guy who didn't heed this warning. He shared everything with his wife. It wasn't long before they couldn't even watch TV together. One evening they were watching ice skating and she said, "I can tell you're lusting after that skater." She changed the channel. Sharing every detail just isn't healthy.

Is Masturbation Okay?

Is there sin that you can commit in your mind? Listen to what Solomon said in Proverbs 5, when he is teaching his son. He says, "Drink water from your own cistern, running water from your own well. Should your springs overflow in the streets, your streams of water in the public squares? Let them be yours alone, never to be shared with strangers" (vv. 15-17). That includes your thoughts.

Masturbation is not an issue of what is going on with you physically—it's about what is going on in your mind. And although both men and women masturbate, it's the guys I've heard talk about it all the time. They say, "The Bible doesn't mention masturbation. It can't be wrong, I need a release." But what's going on in your mind during masturbation? Listen to what Paul says in Colossians 3:5-8:

> Put to death, therefore, whatever belongs to your earthly nature: sexual immorality [that is, sex outside marriage, which is where we get the word "pornography," from *porneia*] impurity, lust [Paul includes not only physical sexual immorality but also *mental* sexual immorality by using the word *pathos*—"lust, lustful passion"], evil desires and greed, which is idolatry. Because of these, the wrath of God is coming. You used to walk in these ways, in the life you once lived. But now you must rid yourself of all such things as these: anger, rage, malice, slander, and filthy language from your lips.

God designed sex for two people, not one. I know it's tough, but you must confess (admit) to God that you are weak and can't stop imagining sex with other women and that you can't stop masturbating. Remember that God "is faithful and just and will forgive us our sins and purify us from all unrighteousness" (1 John 1:9). He alone cleanses you and gives you His freedom through His Holy Spirit and through the power of His living Word. It's God's grace that saves you through faith and not by your works. Let Him give you the section of His Word that you should hide within your heart. Let Him take care of you. That's why His Son died for you and me.

But Is Masturbation Okay When My Spouse and I Cannot Be Together?
Because the Bible offers no direct teaching on this subject, we must apply other biblical principles to help us prayerfully discern God's will for us. So, on the subject of masturbation, a couple should answer four questions:

First, is the self-stimulation harmful to your mutual expectation to be available to one another sexually? If one spouse masturbates instead of being available to the other, he or she is violating the relationship.

Second, is the masturbation associated with lust? This is really the key question. Ask yourself, *Have I received God's freedom to not masturbate? Am I lusting, imagining sex with others, to satisfy my own sexual thrills?* In other words, what level of freedom do you have today? You can be lusting on a number of levels. Pure lust is the desire to have something or someone that is not ours. Self-stimulation often becomes connected with a desire for a person who is not your spouse or for a certain body type that is different from your spouse's, and that is absolutely wrong from God's point of view. It *is* possible for self-stimulation to be a mere physical response to a sexual urge without any thought of anyone, or to be an activity accompanied by images of being with one's spouse. In those situations, there is no lust associated with self-stimulation. But let's be honest: How many men have enough inner strength to lust for just their spouse? If you have it, praise God.

Third, has masturbation become an addiction or enslavement? A person controlled by masturbation is enslaved by or addicted to it. Many behaviors become sin when they enslave a person. In 1 Corinthians 6:12, Paul says, "'Everything is permissible for me'—but I will not be mastered by anything" (see also 1 Cor. 10:23-31).

Fourth, does the masturbation involve self-abuse? Occasionally, people who have been abused in the past may abuse themselves physically or emotionally when they masturbate. This is always wrong. Our bodies are the temple of the Holy Spirit and should be cared for and protected.

We should not be possessed, mastered or enslaved by our sexual drive. Nevertheless, the sexual drive that is in us is natural and God-given. Keeping these two facts in balance will help you and your spouse decide how to think about masturbation in your marriage.

Questions About Married Sex

How Often Is Healthy for a Couple? How Often Should We Do It?
If you are newly married, it will be quite often. I have asked hundreds of senior adults this question in researching this book, and here is what I learned: two or three times a month, but it is hot those two or three times. For middle-aged people, it could be two to three times a week. There are too many variables to give you a mathematical equation.

If you don't nurture the marriage, the oneness and the marital journey, I promise you that sex will get old. Sex will lose its appeal and its excitement. Nurture the relationship, and intimacy will happen automatically.

Don't forget about all the men who have lost the ability to have sex with their mate but can still lust with effective masturbation while imagining someone sexually other than their spouse. Sex lost at any age does not mean the end of the marriage or of all the affectionate activities that come with a good marriage relationship. For me (Gary) at age 68, my wife and I can still be very affectionate toward each other, but because of the medications I've needed since my heart attack and kidney transplant, the ability to have sex is gone.

We have a friend who was telling us that his upcoming operation would result in "the death" of his sex life. Norma responded sadly, "Oh, I'm sorry, but now you'll be like a neutered dog—they're much sweeter after the operation."

He didn't appreciate her comments, but he still smiled.

For me, I'm more thrilled today by watching how God's Word has transformed me and given me the freedom to love others without any more desires to use women in any way through imagining them for my pleasures. I'm truly free to love others by learning how to serve them more than ever before. I feel 40 years old, and each day is a new day to love God and others in new ways.

Is Oral Sex Okay?

Okay? It's phenomenal! Between a husband and wife who are passionately in love, oral sex is one of the greatest gifts in a marriage. But remember that the wife sets the boundaries in the bedroom. Both husband and wife must be comfortable with this exploration.

As our friend Dr. Kevin Leman says, "Mr. Happy likes to be kissed."

Is Anal Sex Okay?

This can be a very dangerous practice. The tissue of the anus is much more sensitive and delicate than that around the vagina. There can be severe medical consequences for engaging in this kind of sexual activity. We advise against it.

An important question to ask of a mate who suggests this type of activity is, "Why?" Is there a lack of creativity? Is there a source outside of the marriage that has planted this seed, such as pornography? There are plenty of ways to bring passion back to your sex life without engaging in anal sex.

Is Viewing Pornography Together as a Couple Okay?

No. Creativity is a big part of sex, as we explored in chapter 9. When sex is viewed as a tool for orgasm and not as a tool for oneness, it loses its excitement, spontaneity and everything that God intended for it to be.

What do you do when the sex life starts to calm down for a couple? Sometimes I (Ted) will hear guys say that they just don't have an interest in sex anymore. Half the time, I don't believe them. If a guy isn't getting a release from his wife, then he's probably getting it from someone else or relieving himself. So sometimes a couple will try to spice things up by adding new imagery to their relationship. They'll rationalize, "Since my body isn't turning you on anymore and your body isn't turning me on anymore or you are not meeting my emotional needs, let's get pornography. Let's go rent a video and watch it together."

But sexual immorality is one of the greatest destroyers of your spiritual growth. You don't want the images of anyone but your spouse in your mind when you're having sex. Think about it. When you're making love to your spouse and the lights are out and your eyes are closed, you don't want your spouse imagining someone else. When you introduce pornography into your marriage, you're introducing an addiction that will undermine your relationship.

Realize that you are not going to develop intimacy as God designed it with your mate if you're thinking about some Hollywood actor or actress. Even soft pornography creates unrealistic expectations that will require an increasing unrealistic expectation to be met. Your mate is not going to be able to keep up with all the cameras, lights and glitz. It's important not to create those unrealistic expectations in the home.

Remember that sex is just a barometer of the marriage. If it is not hot in the bedroom, you don't need to introduce pornography to make it hot in the bedroom. Instead, let me suggest to you some creative things to do. Ladies, take a Polaroid of yourself and leave it somewhere for your husband (just make sure it's a place where only your husband will find it!). This is perfectly okay!

Ladies, dress in the morning in front of him slowly. Don't hide behind the shower. Let him see you dress. Don't rush to get dressed, take your time. At nighttime, candles become your best friend. They can create a warm atmosphere in the room, so you can be comfortable being on display for your husband.

Reread chapter 9 on creativity! Remember that the bedroom is not the only place to make love. The kitchen is a great place. The dining room is a great place. The living room is a great place. Go outside to appropriate places. You can do a lot of things without introducing another couple on video into your lovemaking.

Guys, here is the best way for you to keep it creative: Be responsive outside the bedroom and talk to her. She loves nonsexual touches. Energy and the sex drive are linked.

Is It Okay for My Husband and Me to Film Ourselves Making Love?

We must give a strong caution here. The marriage bed is to be honored and private. So long as the footage is not viewed by anyone else, we can't give you a definite no. However, if there is any chance that it can be viewed by someone else, especially children, then the answer is definitely no. It is better to be safe with this one and go with the no.

How Do I Fight Against Internet Pornography?

There are five ways to regain strength and remain strong so that you don't fall when tempted with lust and Internet pornography.

First, rehearse the negative consequences of sexual involvement, even in the midst of lustful thoughts:

- Loss of trust
- Loss of marriage
- Loss of ministry
- Loss of family
- Irreparable damage to relationships

Second, memorize sections of Scripture that deal specifically with sexual freedom. After memorizing them, persistently ask God to make your life consistent with these verses:

- Matthew 6:13
- Romans 6:6
- 1 Corinthians 10:13
- Colossians 3:5
- 1 Peter 2:11
- 1 Peter 4:2

Third, for men especially, beware of the anger-lust cycle that often develops. Many men experience their most severe times of lust after a struggle or problem at home or at work. Giving in to lust does not break the anger-lust cycle; it only intensifies it. Now not only are you angry and depressed about your problem at work or at home, but you are also angry about your lack of self-control. And on top of your shame, if you are a Christian, you also have the Holy Spirit convicting you of sin. Genuine repentance is a biblical solution, but getting furious with yourself and vowing it will never happen again do little good.

Fourth, get rid of your computer. If you need a computer for work, get filters and allow your pastor, an accountability partner or a small-group leader to do random checks on the history of how you use the machine. Accountability is the key to overcoming this destructive addiction.

Finally, consider starting or joining a support group for those who struggle in this area. It's a long-term process.

Does My Being Addicted to Pornography Give My Mate a Right to Divorce Me?

Addictions can destroy marriages. When a husband is turned on sexually by pornography, the wife feels unwanted, unattractive, rejected, abandoned—the list of emotions could go on and on. Your self-gratification from your sexual addiction has lessened your desire for your wife. Women crave emotional connection from their husbands. Your wife has no connection with you. I share all this so that you can see how damaging your addiction is to your marriage. You must seek help and accountability for your addiction so that your marriage can begin a healing process.

Matthew 19:9 teaches us that divorce is wrong "except for marital unfaithfulness." The word there for "marital unfaithfulness" is *porneia*. It means physical adultery that is persistent, relentless and unrepentant. Lust has never been listed in Scripture as grounds for divorce.

For now, avoiding divorce should not be your goal. Getting healthy should be your first priority. Work on yourself before you work on getting your wife back. Refuse to point the finger of blame at your spouse or anyone else. No one but you is at fault for your addiction.

With God's help, you can kick this. Willpower will not work. You need the power of Christ flowing through you. You can do all things through Christ who gives you strength (see Phil. 4:13).

Start with yourself, and then work on your marriage.

I Grew Up in a Home Where Even the Mention of the Word "Sex" Was Forbidden. How Do I Develop a Healthy Perspective on Sex?

In an attempt to protect their children's virginity, some parents fall into the trap of using shame-based sex education. They use code words, minimal details and shyness to address the issue of sex. This sort of education often results in a belief that sex is unmentionable or even dirty.

God is holy. God created sex. He designed sex. He wants you to enjoy it. As a pastor, I am deeply concerned about the sex life of each family member at our church. I want each church member to have great sex in God's context. The couples in our church that enjoy mutually satisfying great sex naturally have strong marriages.

Here are four steps you can take to develop healthy beliefs about sex.

1. *Start reading.* You've already started this by reading through this book. Hopefully, you have now discovered truths about sexual intimacy straight from Scripture that you never knew before.

2. *Start talking.* Begin with your spouse or future spouse. Talk to your kids. Discuss sexual intimacy with trusted friends or within a Bible study. Healthy discussion fosters healthy beliefs.

3. *Stop the silence.* We must reclaim sex as a topic to be discussed by churches and parents, not Hollywood or the schools.

4. *Seek pastoral or professional help.* Your beliefs may need more help than a few books or friends can provide. Take the risk and seek out good, biblical instruction.

How Do We Approach Our Kids with the Topic of Sex?

I think the best way to approach kids with the subject of sex is with prayer, grace, love and honesty. All too often parents fall into the unhealthy pattern of using code words, a practice usually started when kids are young.

My four-year-old, Corynn, asks a lot of questions and some of them deal with sexuality. She will ask, "What is that on Carson?" Rather than use terms like "pee-pee," "woo-hoo" or "wah-wah," I tell her, "That's your brother's penis."

It's important to understand and communicate what's appropriate and what's not. But when we start using code names and trying to hide the truth behind the birds and the bees and all of that, we rob our children of knowing the truth and becoming comfortable with who they are and who God has created them to be.

Recently my daughter and I were taking a walk, when she piped up, "She's a girl too, right, Daddy?"

"Yeah, she's a girl," I confirmed.

"She has breasts. I don't have those," she said.

"Well, one day I will buy you a training bra!" I responded. "Won't that be exciting on the day your breasts start forming? That will happen in about 10 years."

Now my daughter doesn't know the difference between 10 years and 10 minutes, so she keeps checking to see if she's getting close. I tell her it's a long way down the road.

During preschool, a child's brain is developing rapidly. If you teach such young children that their bodies are shameful things, and you do that in the most subtle ways, then they'll believe that for years to come. That's why it's so important to avoid code names and to be honest with your children.

Note

1. Richard Dobbins, "Bonding," *Homemade* (November 1987), quoted at Bible.org, 2007. http://www.bible.org/illus.php?topic_id=1392 (accessed August 24, 2007).

The Smalley Relationship Center provides conferences and resources for couples, singles, parents, and churches. The Center captures research, connecting to your practical needs and develops new tools for building relationships.

resources include:

- Over 50 best-selling books on relationships
- Small Group curriculums on marriage & parenting
- Church-wide campaign series with sermon series, daily emails and much more
- Video/DVD series
- Newlywed kit and pre-marital resources

www.garysmalley.com website includes:

- Over 300 articles on practical relationship topics
- Weekly key truths on practical issues
- Daily devotionals
- Conference dates and locations
- Special events
- Weekly newsletter
- Free personality & core fear profiles
- Request a SRC Speaker

To find out more about Gary Smalley's speaking schedule, conferences, and to receive a weekly e-letter with articles and coaching ideas on your relationships, go to www.garysmalley.com or call 1.800.8486329

Attend our live **I Promise Marriage Seminars** taught by

DRS. GARY & GREG
SMALLEY

A six session marriage seminar based on the new
I Promise book and Purpose Driven Curriculum

Free Resources: go to **www.garysmalley.com**

- **Weekly E-letter**

  Receive articles, coaching tips and, inspirational encouragement
  from Gary Smalley which will help you build a more effective and
  stronger marriage.

- **Profiles** ①

  The overall theme of I Promise is security, and you can take a 20 question test on how secure your most important relationship is.

  (Bonus: After you take that profile consider taking our personality
  profile which gives you even more insight into what kind of
  personality styles you andyour spouse fall into.)

Sign up for our FREE
@E-LETTER
WWW.GARYSMALLEY.COM

IN OUR E-LETTER, YOU'LL RECEIVE THE FOLLOWING:

Articles
[Over 300 articles on practical relationship topics]

Key Truths
[Weekly Key Truths on practical issues]

Devos
[Fresh Daily Devotion each day]

Dates & Locations
[Where & when our Seminars are held]

Special Events
[Conferences, Speaking Events, etc.]

Assessments
[Go online to take our free personality and core fear profiles]

Speakers
[Request an SRC Speaker]